SPINNING INTO FORM

MARION EATON

A meditative journey through
the seven major chakras.

Copyright © 2014 Marion L. Eaton

The right of Marion L. Eaton to be identified as the author of this work has been asserted by her in accordance with the Copyright, Designs and Patents Act 1988. May all who read this book be richly blessed.

Published by Touchworks Ltd.
a company registered in England, no. 03668464.
Registered Office: 67 London Road, St. Leonards-on-Sea,
East Sussex TN37 6AR.

All rights reserved.
No part of this publication may be reproduced, stored in a retrieval system, or transmitted, in any form or by any means, electronic, mechanical, photocopying, recording or otherwise, without the prior permission of the copyright owner.

A catalogue record for this title is available from the British Library.
Mp3 downloads available from cd.baby.com.
Compact Disks available from amazon.com.

Also by M L Eaton

Mysterious Marsh series
#1 When the Clocks Stopped
#2 When the Tide Turned

Novellas
The Elephants' Choice
Norfolk Twilight

All books available in print and as e-books from Amazon including amazon.co.uk, amazon.com, amazon.com.au and amazon.in.

- For -

My teachers, students, readers and listeners

Thank you all

'When mind knows, we call it knowledge.

When heart knows, we call it love.

And when being knows, we call it

meditation.'

Osho

1

How to use this book

Although this book will tell you a little about subtle energy and the chakra system, it is primarily intended to introduce a simple way of *experiencing* the chakras, those wonderful swirling centres of energy which are our method of communicating on the subtle planes with the world about us.

The book opens with a short explanation of the way that energy spins into matter and then gives a simplified description of the subtle energy body. Following this are short chapters relating to each of the seven major chakras and introducing a way of experiencing them through light meditation. I believe this to be the easiest way to lull the body-mind-spirit into awareness of these centres.

Starting from the base chakra, at the base of the spine, and working upwards these elements are:

Base chakra:	Earth,
Sacral chakra:	Water,
Solar Plexus chakra:	Fire,
Heart chakra:	Air,
Throat chakra:	Ether,
Brow chakra:	Light,
Crown chakra:	Spirit.

Simply reading the mediations slowly, whether silently or aloud, will have a balancing effect on your energy field. They will have a deeper effect if, as you read, you take time to experience the feelings invoked, whether you read them for yourself or to others.

When you have read a meditation once, just keep doing it whenever you can — until, eventually, you experience the energy of the chakra.

Now you will begin to realise when a chakra feels out of balance, or when its losing power, or is working too slowly — or too fast. Often, all you need to do then is to use the breath to bring your awareness to that chakra, or you can work again with the appropriate individual meditation, or the whole *Journey through the Chakras.*

Personally, I prefer to listen to guided meditations rather than to read them. For this reason I have narrated them as a series of short ones — lasting a little over ten minutes each — and as one long meditation that takes approximately an hour.

The following recordings are available to purchase online: for compact discs go to www.amazon.com. Mp3 downloads are available from www.cdbaby.com.

Earth to Air — short meditations on the Earth, Water, Fire and Air,

Ether to Spirit — slightly longer meditations on Ether, Light and Spirit

Spinning into Form — an hour's journey through the chakras.

SPINNING into FORM

To recap, the meditations set out in this book are designed to encourage you to use your breath to take you into an altered state of consciousness where you can open your awareness of the individual elements to which each of the main seven chakras have an affinity.

Whether you read them in print or listen to them in voice form, it is my sincere wish that they may lead you to a place of calm, serenity and wholeness.

Om shanti: may peace be with you.
Namasté: the Divine in me sees the Divine in you.

2

Introduction

For a long time, I thought of writing about the chakras.

But simply writing about them seemed insufficient. I asked myself a question. Could I find a way to *experience* the chakras as living energy?

Eventually, after much experimentation, I found that a meditation connecting the different energies of the chakras with the elements traditionally associated with them, actually worked *for me*. I found that the chakras ceased to be a purely mental construct and became wonderful, multi-faceted, multi-dimensional whirling centres of energy.

I appreciate that this experience is unlikely be the same for all who use these meditations, but I hope that you will find them beneficial, and that they will prove a blessing to you, however small.

As a Holistic Health Practitioner and a teaching Reiki Master for over twenty years, I know that using the chakras as a guide enriches the practice of all healing modalities, whether you are seeking to heal yourself or to assist others in healing themselves.

Although I have learned a great deal about the subtle energy system as I've travelled my Reiki path, I well

4

remember the bafflement I felt when it was first described to me. In those long-ago days, I was a practising lawyer and used to rational ideas and explanations, so I found the whole concept of energy difficult to understand.

Since then, of course, the internet has made information available as never before and the understanding of metaphysical concepts through the medium of quantum physics has blossomed. However, although there is a great deal of information available, it is not always understandable.

Now, before I teach a first Reiki class, I ask my students to come to a workshop in which I outline the subtle energy body and its subtle energy channels, so that when they come to practice this wonderful healing art, they have some understanding and experience of the way that energy spins into matter. In this way, they become aware, not only of subtle energy itself, but of its interaction with the whole of creation.

Although I came to this way of understanding the chakras through Reiki, my intention is that this book of meditations and its accompanying CD or mp3 files will encourage you to experiment and so come to a personal awareness of the chakras and their relevance to everyday life.

3

Trust and Inner Knowing

The first step in understanding our subtle energy is to learn to trust our inner knowledge.

This can be difficult because we've been conditioned by society to trust only what we are taught by others and to hide all those parts of us which we believe to be unacceptable to society. So let's take a long hard look within, imagining we are seeing with the all-seeing Eye. This Eye sees everything within the compass of our body-mind-spirit — our hopes and fears, our happinesses and sadnesses, our kindnesses and cruelties, joys and griefs, wellness and illness, and everything else that we like to keep hidden.

The Eye sees without judging, but with compassion. It looks deeply within, seeing where we are lost, where we are selling ourselves short, where we are stuck in our thought processes, where we are clinging to a belief system that is harmful or weakening. Compassion sees and, in seeing, understands.

From this understanding, we humans have a choice which comes from our free-will. We can stay as we are or we can choose to change, and take responsibility for all that we are — including our feelings, our beliefs and our judgements.

If we choose to change, the change occurs spontaneously.

If we choose to stay as we are, limited by our existing patterns, beliefs and thought forms, there is no judgement. But there is acceptance — and in that acceptance there is also compassion. And that is a kind of change.

Once we accept ourselves, exactly as we are, we can move on — if we want, there is no compulsion — to seeing what serves us and what does not. From there, it is only a short step to deciding what we would like to keep and what we would like to fall away.

This sounds easy, but can be uncomfortable, especially if we realise that the things we need to let go are things, beliefs or people to which we are attached. For this reason we need to be gentle with ourselves, giving ourselves time and encouragement as well as understanding. If you find difficulty in letting go, try blessing each thought, idea or belief — with gratitude for what it has taught you — before releasing it.

4

The Macrocosm - the Cosmos

'In the beginning was the word. The word was with God and the word was God.'

'Om - the sound of the universe.'

'The Big Bang.'

It all began with sound, whether you take as your text the Bible, the ancient Indian scriptures, Chinese metaphysical thinking or modern science.

In the beginning there was a sound and that sound continues to reverberate throughout the cosmos. Sound is the great creator, its vibrations spread and gather and return to the beginning only to be recreated: so the cycle continues.

Sound is vibration. Vibration is sound.

As the sound of the universe swelled and grew and created particles, those particles began to cling together, forming larger particles that in turn found a belonging together, and those particles found an affinity with other particles. Particles continued to clump together until we have the cosmos that we know today.

Everything of which we are aware had its seed in that first vibration of sound.

SPINNING into FORM

But it did not stop there, with the Creation: for sound, the creator, is also the destroyer. As sound swells and dies, so do we humans grow and fade — as does everything else that has its being in the Cosmos. As particles cling together, so they part and return to the matrix from which all is created and re-created.

Change, movement and energy are the only constants.

We are limited by our human senses. Whilst we are aware that our ears pick up certain sounds, we know that there are sounds of both higher and lower vibrations that our sense of hearing cannot discern. Thus we speak of 'ultra-sound' when we mean a sound that our human ears cannot hear. We accept that there are different levels of hearing: not only does human hearing vary from individual to individual, but we are aware that dogs, animals and insects pick up different frequencies from those of which we humans are aware.

The sounds we hear with our ears are those that travel comparatively slowly, because we can only pick up sounds of certain frequencies. Very low sounds are beneath our perception. As the frequency speeds up, the sound moves beyond our human capacity to hear with our ears: at higher frequencies we see vibration as light.

Light is vibration. Vibration is light.

Light is sound speeded up, travelling faster than the human ear or eye can follow. For years it was thought that light was the fastest vibration in the cosmos, but now it has been proved that this is not the case.

There is a faster dimension. One that we can seldom discern within our bodies, but of which our living being — our body-mind-spirit — is aware. Those things we see with our inner eyes when our physical eyes are closed, those vibrations we pick up from the world about us — vibrations of which our senses are unaware — these are reverberations of the 'First Sound' thrumming through our being.

There are faster dimensions still: many are just being discovered as scientists unravel 'the field' in which we all have our being. Now it is known that there is no single universe but a multiverse of different dimensions. Now scientist and meta-physicist alike accept that we do not live in a world of three — or possibly four — dimensions as had been previously thought. We live in a multi-dimensional world, scientists now agreeing that there are eleven or twelve dimensions to our cosmos. This resonates with centuries-old Buddhist teachings and long before that, much was understood in ancient India, although only put into writing much later in time.

For those of us who seek to find more than the physical world around us, who feel that Life is greater than a single life on earth, who seek answers to the many facets of life of which we are aware but know not how — now is the time of awakening to that inner knowing.

5

The Microcosm - the human

Sound is a form of energy. Light is a form of energy. The earth is a form of energy. Plants are a form of energy. Animals are a form of energy. We humans are a form of energy.

Although we seem to be individuals in our own right, solid flesh and warm blood, in fact we are pure energy. We can recognise our thoughts as energy because they have no physical form, but it is much more difficult to see our individual bodies as nothing but vibrating energy. However, this is a fact. A fact which has been recognised by metaphysical thinkers and knowers for millennia: and — perhaps more importantly to those of us who are alive here and now — a fact which modern scientists and physicists also proclaim.

In the beginning was the word — or the twinkle in your father's eye, or the immense longing of your mother for a child. In the beginning there was ENERGY. From this word, longing or twinkle emanated a being in its own right. First, the new being was simply a cell. A cell that used its energy to divide itself into two, according to the energetic pattern set down in its DNA — and then to replicate its cells into ever larger and more elaborate patterns and organs until over the course of nine months or so, a baby is born that holds within its small person the blueprint and energy of the adult it will become.

The pattern is set down in an acid that is contained within the baby's cells. DNA (deoxyribonucleic acid, a self-replicating material which is present in nearly all living organisms as the main constituent of chromosomes) is the shortened name by which we know this amazing structure of genes, so small that it is impossible to perceive with the naked eye, so specific that there is less than one chance in a million that someone else will have the same DNA pattern as you — unless you are an identical twin when the possibilities are much higher. The mitochondrial DNA passed down by the mother of a child seldom alters over the centuries. For this reason it is possible to find descendants of a known woman often millennia after she has lived. However, the paternal offering is different, varying from child to child. The fascinating result is that when both parts join, the combined DNA pattern is unique to each individual.

It is well known that DNA is a double helix, spiralling round and twisted in upon itself, confined within a tiny space in each cell. The amazing reality is that, when stretched out, a single DNA strand measures a little over a metre — yet it is contained within the tiny nucleus of a cell that itself is invisible to the human eye. The only way to store this information within a cell is to contain it within a

SPINNING into FORM

spiralling structure. This remarkable discovery — which was only made in the middle of the twentieth century — is now common knowledge.

It is this common knowledge which makes it easier to understand that energy, and thus the information it contains, is constantly in motion, spiralling through every atom and nano-particle in the cosmos. As energy spirals into form it travels in an anti-clockwise direction — the constructive cycle — but as it dissipates and moves out of form its polarity is reversed and it spins clockwise — the destructive cycle.

This constant spiralling movement, as things spin into form and then out again into formless energy, is illustrated by what happens in Nature. Each year, a plant will put out shoots, grow, flower, fruit, seed, die back and decay. The length of the process is different for each living thing, but this is the inevitable way of energy — constantly giving and constantly taking away. If this did *not* happen, the world could not exist as it is today. It would be full of the things that had not decayed. And the bacteria and fungi that feed on dead matter would have no function and no life.

As the process of Life continues, other factors begin to have a bearing on our cells. The usual factors are our thoughts and emotions, but nutrients, air, water, accidents and other apparently random events have an effect as well. Slowly our cells themselves change. And this means that they produce slightly different cells when they reproduce before they die — a process called apoptosis.

But I digress. Let me take you back to the spiralling form of energy: the Goddess' spiral of construction. Energy spins anti-clockwise as it comes in from the cosmos and permeates every fibre, every cell, every tiny space within our cells. This energy, is strong and loving and it contains all the information in the universe.

In spinning into form, we have ceased to be creatures simply 'of Spirit'. We have taken the decision to come to Earth and in order to do so it is essential to clothe our beautiful spiritual soul -energy in a physical body.

The vibration of the physical body is comparatively dense and gross. To exist, live and move this form requires a completely different set of attributes — skin, limbs, organs, skeleton etc — but also organs of knowledge and thought, spiritual senses and a range of intuitions and emotions to guide it through the maze of Life.

6

Spinning into Form

As science has now ascertained, we humans (and all other living things) are far more than a physical body and a thinking mind. We are all living beings with an individualised energy field which makes us distinct from the energies surrounding us. However, essentially we are not separate, since we are all part of the living energy matrix that surrounds the planet and envelops the whole cosmos.

Urbanised creatures that we have become, we may find it difficult to comprehend that we are essentially a full and functioning part of Nature. We are dependent on Nature for everything that we have. No matter how clever we become at manufacturing 'man-made' goods, every single substance from which those goods are constructed comes from, and is a part of, the planet on which we live.

We are dependent on the atmosphere to protect us from the strength of the sun's rays, on gravity to keep us secure on the Earth's surface, and other living organisms for the ability to continue to live. These include the bacteria on our skin that keeps our epidermis healthy; the bacteria in our intestines that produce our B vitamins, and the plants that clean and oxygenate the air that we breathe. We are dependent on the oceans for the weather, for food and for the water in our cells; on the animals that provide us with food and warmth and that keep the planet's ecosystem in balance. The whole of life is dependent on the whole of life: a truth which brings us back to the beginning and to the life force energy that permeates all things.

When the 'Big Bang' occurred, energy began to spiral outwards and that spiralling has never stopped from that moment onward. All energy is vibrant. All particles spin and move and constantly change.

In truth, change and movement are the only two constants in existence. The rates of change and movement may vary, but the essential constants do not.

The ancients understood this property of energy. They looked at the clouds and saw them move, they watched the spiralling currents in water and the way the rivers zig-zagged along their courses, they watched the ever-changing night skies and understood the procession of the stars and planets and the changing course of the sun. They recognised these things so well that they were able to build huge monuments like Stonehenge in England, the round towers in Ireland and the Pyramids of Egypt, all of which act as almanacs for the sun and stars.

Most important of all, they recognised that we are of the stars, made of the same substance as all of Life. Today, science recognises the truth of these observations and adds its own interpretations of the subject matter.

Although energy is constantly in motion, it never moves in a straight line. Always there is some spiralling movement along a line's length. The Earth's energy spirals like a snake or dragon and for this reason the creatures themselves were, and in several cultures still are, honoured and considered sacred. The song lines of Australia, the green hollow roads of England and the great labyrinths of the world from Nebraska to Chartres Cathedral, all move in a spiralling motion from the outside to the centre and from the centre back to the outside.

7

The Aura

If all the energy-information in the cosmos were available to us, our senses would experience overload and would be unable to function. For this reason we have a range of filters that process this energy-information.

The first of these filters is known in poetic Sanskrit as 'the aura'. In modern 'scientific speak' it is called 'the electro-magnetic sheath' but I will use the term *aura* to describe it.

Both ancient wisdom and modern science agree that the aura is a roughly egg-shaped envelope of energy of a fairly low electro-magnetic frequency that surrounds the physical body. Many factors – such as the health of the person, her awareness, her emotional and spiritual state, the nature of her personality and mood and her physical surroundings — affect the aura's size and efficacy.

The Auric Membrane:

Surrounding and containing an individual's aura is a strong, fine membrane that protects the stepped-down energy layers within. This membrane's function is to prevent certain energy-information — usually energy that is either of too high or of too low a frequency for the individual to bear — from entering the individual's electro magnetic field.

As energy is filtered into the auric system, the body-mind-spirit is continually adjusting to the information that energy contains. (Please note that I use the term 'body-mind-spirit' because it is clear that we are more than a physical body. We have beliefs, thoughts, aspirations and emotions that, in their totality, are unique to us; and they are all contained within our individual auric field.)

If a person's auric membrane is damaged or distressed, he or she is likely to suffer from spiritual, mental, emotional or physical problems.

The Auric Layers/Bodies:

We have already seen that the aura itself is subject to change. So, too, are the several layers of energy within the aura. These layers (often known as *bodies*) are formed as the frequency of the energy is gradually lowered on its way into the physical body. This system of layers is often described as similar to a series of Russian dolls that nest inside each other, but this analogy is flawed because there are no finite boundaries surrounding the auric layers. Each energy-frequency interpenetrates the others and all interpenetrate the physical body.

The Spiritual Body:

The layer of the human aura that contains spiritual understanding vibrates the fastest and thus can be sensed further away from the physical body-mind-spirit than layers of lower frequencies. Remember, though, that its vibration interpenetrates the person's whole being.

The Mental Body:

Much more dense in vibration is the auric layer of the mind: our thoughts. Thoughts are strong energy: so strong, in fact, that they can bend and mark a person's whole being. In this form they are often referred to collectively as 'the ego'.

The Emotional Body:

Close to this mental layer, and intimately linked with it, is the layer of our emotions. Thoughts and emotions are so interconnected that they constantly affect each other. For this reason this auric layer/level of energy is often considered as being joined with the layer of mind: 'the mental-emotional field.'

The Etheric Body:

Last of the auric layers is 'the etheric body'. Often seen as a thin bluish haze around the physical body, this is the energy 'blueprint' for the physical body and the field most easily seen with our physical eyes.

The Ten Long Currents

Inside all these inter-connected auric layers, the energy is not still: it is a swirling, spiralling mass of information. But as it enters the physical body the energy becomes more cohesive, running in streams through the etheric body. The Indian sages realised that these streams of a high frequency energy run along ten channels that encircle the physical body. Five streams on each side of the physical body run through the head and trunk (including the main organs) as well as through the limbs, fingers and toes. On the left side of the body they pass up the front and down the back, while on the right side the flow is reversed, running down the front and up the back.

The Meridians:

As their frequency reduces, these streams become both more confined and more defined. In the physical body they can be mapped precisely, and were named 'meridians' by Chinese scholars and 'nadis' by Indian guru-philosophers.

The Sushumna:

At the same time, spiritual energy from the cosmos streams down from the crown of the head through a central channel along the line of the spine, to the pelvic floor. From there it descends into the earth. This channel is called the 'Sushumna'. Through it, the energy of the universe is earthed. When the energy of the Sushumna reaches the earth, its polarity is reversed, and runs from the earth up the spine and out into the universe.

The Ida and Pingala:

On either side of the Sushumna channel are two spiralling energy lines known as the 'Ida' and 'Pingala'. They run from the nostrils to the base of the spine, and from the base of the spine upward. The Pingala is masculine and hot: the Ida is feminine and cold. These spiralling energies cross at various points along the spinal matrix and in those places they also interconnect with the energy centres that are known as 'chakras'.

These are not the only energy paths in the human body-mind-spirit that have been mapped by physicists and meta-physicists alike, but to include reference to more than those given above is beyond the scope of this book.

8

The Chakras

'Chakra' is a Sanskrit word and its meaning is usually translated as 'wheel'. This word indicates the continuous spiralling whirling nature of the energy at these centres; centres which are the energy interface between our body-mind-spirit and our surroundings. The chakras are the vehicles that collect, interpret and deal with the information and power that is available to us through the energy that is processed here.

We seldom give a thought to the fact that we possess information about the world around us long before we react to that information. When we are in conversation with someone else, the words that he speaks account only for approximately seven per cent of the information we pick up about him. Long before he has finished speaking, we have processed his size and shape, his emotional baggage, his intentions, his feelings about the matter, the truth of what he is saying, whether he is lying, what we intuit he really wishes to say and some understanding of how his words relate to his spiritual belief system.

The way that we process this information is through our chakras.

We might say: 'I have a gut feeling about this...' What

we are inferring is that we have an emotional reaction (Sacral chakra) to whatever it might be. Again, we might acknowledge that 'His heart is not in it,' (Heart chakra) meaning that we are aware that he is not truly happy or committed.

I will pay more attention to the individual chakras in the chapters dedicated to them, but first we need to be aware that as energy slows it becomes denser. Thus the vibration of the bones in our bodies is much slower, and the frequency lower, than in the liver or the skin.

The highest vibrational energy (approximately 2,500 hertz) has been measured in the crown chakra: the lowest (approximately 250 hertz) in the base chakra. As energy is stepped down at each chakra, the vibration rate becomes slower, so that the fastest spiritual energy whirls at the Crown chakra while the densest, most physical energy is found in the Base chakra.

Specific frequencies above the frequency of the Crown chakra have been measured by scientists. These are the frequencies of meditation and evolve as the meditator raises his consciousness towards the Infinite.

The wonderful truth is that we have power over our own energy: and that power is exercised by our intention — by simply making a choice.

So without more ado, let's look a little more closely at the whirling centres of energy known as chakras.

SPINNING into FORM

Many have written more eloquently than I about the individual chakras and I do not intend to go into detail here: that is beyond the purpose of this little book and its accompanying meditations, which is to lead you gently into *experiencing* the chakras through the medium of the elements connected with them.

The chakras are invisible to all but a few people, but that does not mean that they are not powerful. Quite the reverse. They exercise a powerful pull and impact on our mental-emotional-physical selves.

We are seldom aware of a chakra's impact on our physical energy. Often the only thing we notice is that we are feeling 'out-of-sorts', or nervous, or apprehensive. Sometimes this feeling is reflected in part of the body. Sometimes we feel nauseated, or sick, or unable to eat. Perhaps we are tearful and 'choked', maybe we feel dizzy, or have a headache. These symptoms can present themselves suddenly or appear over a period of time. All are indications of a chakra out of balance.

In my experience, it is by becoming aware of how a chakra feels when it is *in* balance and functioning well, that we are able to notice when that chakra is out of balance and that we need to pay it more attention. So I believe it important to gather a *feeling* for each individual chakra.

When a chakra is balanced it is spinning happily, giving and receiving information from the whole cosmos in general and from our own aura and our other chakras in particular.

All chakras have an affinity with the organs and endocrine glands that are close to them, but I do not intend to go deeply into these relationships.

Once you experience the feeling of the chakra the rest will follow naturally. You will find yourself the owner of personal wisdom and understanding that you had no idea was available to you.

If there is one single thing that I hope you find within these meditations it is that you have access to far more understanding, inner knowing and intuition than you have believed possible before. Too often we are brought up to believe that we know nothing unless our knowledge is garnered from books.

But all knowledge that is contained in other people's writings — including these — is from the writer's own mind. Their own thoughts, in fact. Or the thoughts of others re-worded and re-distilled.

You are so much more than that.

You are the essence of all mankind. Each of us is aware and open to all the knowledge in the universe and beyond. Our physical body, our brains and our thinking mind can only hold a microscopic amount of the information and knowledge available to us. Beyond the little 'self' is a huge self that has access to the whole, to All-That-Is. We are here on Earth to use the gifts we are given in this earthly life to discern those things that will make our lives full, happy and contented, useful to the cosmos and a gift to all Beings.

First we must throw away the trappings of our education and the belief systems that we have inherited or taken on from others. Only then are we ready to experience life in all its richness exactly as we were designed to do, and in the way that was ordained for us when we clothed our spirits in flesh and came down to this Earth.

We are here to be ourselves, truly ourselves; and in doing so to raise the vibrational level of all Life, not only on this planet but everywhere.

So throw out all that you think you know — and experiment! Take yourself back to the day you were born. Perfect, a blank canvas on which Life has yet to be written. Allow yourself to forget all that you have learned from books, people, your environment, your family, teachers and gurus. You are your own guru. You have the power to choose your own belief system. You have the power to experiment with all that the chakras, in their magnificent simplicity, have to offer, and to learn — whatever your wishes and needs — from the process.

I will give only the most basic information on the seven major chakras so that you know the area to which you should give your attention as you follow the meditations.

9

Three Tips for Meditation

Three small tips to help with any meditation.

1.   Before you begin, EITHER stretch and relax each part of your body in turn, starting from the feet. Don't forget your face! Screw it up and then release. OR shake from top to bottom, continuing to do so for at least 2 minutes, remembering to shake your feet, and your jaw. Shake out all tension.

THEN release any tension in your pelvic floor and any tension in your jaw, smile a little, feel the muscles of your face relax.

2.   Listen outwards with your ears. Actively listen to all sounds you can hear outside your body — outside the room, beyond the property's boundaries.

Stretch and lengthen your hearing and you will find that your body naturally finds a dynamic state of stillness and your breath calms and becomes light and even.

3.   Allow your body to become completely still as you sit or lie comfortably with your back straight. Keep still. Stillness will hold your meditation calmly in place.

10

EARTH - Base Chakra

The base chakra is situated at the bottom of the energy channel known as the Sushumna near the base of the spine. It spills out from the pelvic floor between the sex organs and the anus. General wisdom has it that the chakra spins downwards towards the ground. The slowest of the seven major chakras, its frequency is close to the magnetic field of the Earth.

Thus, the element to which this chakra relates is Earth, and the sense connected with it is the sense of smell. Its main function is of elimination, but we should always remember that all the atoms of our being are made from substances that come from this planet and that when we die, whether we are cremated or buried, our atoms will return to the Earth: "dust to dust, ashes to ashes," in the words of the psalm used in Christian funerals.

When we excrete, whether faeces, urine, breath or thoughts, our excretions return to the world around us. Our excrement and urine is needed to support other forms of life that, in turn, support us. The beetles and bacteria that live on our waste matter process it into forms available to other units of life, making it available to plants which use it to grow. From our waste matter, plants fashion wonderful cool green cathedrals for our refreshment and food for us to eat, not to mention the oxygen on which our breath depends. Life supports Life.

And this is another wheel of which we should be cognisant.

Here are three simple ways to experience the Base Chakra by bringing your conscious awareness to it. Some take longer than others but all can be accomplished within fifteen minutes. Choose the one that appeals to you most at any given time.

Remember that you may not merge into the Oneness every time you meditate. Indeed it may take a few tries before your mind settles sufficiently to trust the process. And your body too — it is probably unused to stillness.

ONE

A few breaths will help to steady and calm you whatever you are doing or thinking. You may stop doing or thinking … or you may breathe consciously as you carry on with your daily tasks.

A single conscious breath will work wonders: more slow conscious breaths will calm and relax you and clarify your thinking.

TWO

Breathe out fully … breathe in deeply … hold the breath … and let it go. Breathe out as much as you are able and then breathe out a little more ... breathe in ... and smile! Keep breathing, letting your breath find its own rhythm. Smile deeply into your Base Chakra, accept its gifts and relax. See if any sensations or thoughts drift into your mind ... let them be ... Let nothing change ... only your awareness. Let your awareness linger at your pelvic floor, near the base of your spine ... smile into that chakra.

That is all. You can stay here for as long as you wish, drifting on the breath, staying comfortably aware of this vital part of yourself.

Or you may wish to use the breath to bring yourself back into everyday consciousness, allowing your awareness to come back to your surroundings.

It is simply a choice. Your choice.

THREE

A guided meditation, like the one below, is a simple way to find a sense of Oneness if you have 10 to 15 minutes to spare for meditation.

If you wish, you can choose to listen to my voice as it carries you into an awareness of Earth and an understanding of the groundedness and security connected with this chakra.

EARTH MEDITATION
Base Chakra

Sit or lie with your back straight. If your back is sore you may lie with a pillow under your knees to take the pressure from your back. Make sure you are comfortable. Stretch and relax each part of your body in turn. If you become aware of tension, take your full attention to that part. Breathe into it. Do not try to change anything. Just allow the tension to be there, acknowledge it and move on.

Take a deep slow breath … and as you breathe out slowly and deeply, become aware of the breath as it passes warmly through your nostrils. As you breathe in feel the slight coolness of the breath and follow it on its journey to your centre. As you breathe out, note its warmth … as you breathe in, note its coolness. Allow the breath to follow its natural pattern …. There is nothing to achieve other than awareness of the breath. There is nothing to do but follow the breath on its slow passage …. In …. And out …. Good.

Allow your breath to become lighter … silent. With each out-breath feel your whole body becoming heavy, heavy, heavy … and relaxed…. Your whole body is relaxed and at ease. Your body is warm: warm and heavy. Heavy and warm … and relaxed.

As you breath out, acknowledge the floor beneath you. Become aware of the places where the floor and your

SPINNING into FORM

body meet. Allow yourself to become one with the floor. Breathe in and breathe out. Softly. Lightly.

Feel your heavy, warm, body sinking into the floor … becoming one with the floor.

As you become one with the floor, allow your body to melt into it. And become aware that the floor has changed its texture. It is warm and it is soft. It is mud … Earth: warm, soft, supportive Earth. Feel how it holds you … supports you … nourishes you … like a mother holding her child warmly to her breast.

Feel the sensation of the Earth against your skin.

Now become aware of the smell of the Earth: the soft muddy odour of the Earth after rain; the intense primeval smell.

Feel the scent all around you, soaking your own scent up from your skin.

Let yourself become aware of the taste of the Earth: so close to its smell… As you breathe in the scent, hold its taste on your tongue ….

Feel relaxed … relaxed and warm and Earthy…..

Hear the small sounds of the Earth: soft, sticky sounds perhaps. Or the dry flicking sound of dust. Allow your sense of hearing to become very still … very acute … very clear.

Hear the sound of water deep within the Earth: the sound of plant roots growing down into the Earth: Listen to the movement of each infinitesimally small insect and each tiny worm.

See with your inner eye the texture of the Earth. It may be soft, slimy mud: it may be hard and dusty. Or it may be a warm, fine, tilth just ready for the seed to be planted.

However it is for you, take time to look at it closely, so that you become aware of the micro-organisms that comprise it: the soil, the Earth.

Now allow all those sensations to merge in your mind … in your inner being … in your emotions. Sense the feeling, the living being, that is Earth.

Allow your awareness to encompass all that Earth means to you. Whether that is the joy of lying on it on a warm summer's day; or striding through muddy puddles on a walk down a farm track. Whether it is striding up a hill, or climbing a mountain. Clinging to rocks, or running barefoot in the sand. Digging a flowerbed, or making mud pies as a child.

Be a child! Play with the Earth in any way that takes your fancy. Taste it; chew it; smooth it with your hands, your toes. Make mud pies … or sandcastles. Rub dirt into your hair. Let soil dribble through your fingers … allow it to become soft and bathe in it. Smear it all over your skin … smother yourself in mud. Do any, or all, of these things; or find your own fun. Use it laughingly and with joy and feel the sheer wonder of its existence.

Be aware that Earth is the foundation of all life. We

SPINNING into FORM

are truly children of the Earth.

… Give yourself all the time you need to truly experience Earth in this moment. And then — when you are ready — take a moment to give thanks. To acknowledge … to remember … that the Earth takes all our negativity; takes all our unnecessary waste; the manure of our bodies; the toxicity of our emotions — and sanitises them. Commutes them, and transforms them to soil in which beautiful plants can grow.

Let go of all your negativity … physical … mental … emotional. Let it seep into the Earth for transformation, transmutation. Into the Earth, with gratitude. Leaving you happy and clean, clear of all negativity.

If you feel dirty or muddy, you may need a shower. Or a bath. Under a waterfall, in a deep pool. Whatever your needs, allow yourself to emerge shining clean. Full of delight: delightful. Full of joy: joyful.

… Hold that feeling: knowledge; deep knowing; understanding. And now simply accept, know … and understand … on all the levels of your being — from the superficial to the deepest core — that the Earth accepts you as you are. There is nothing you have to do … or be … or achieve.

With all your imperfections, you are perfect as you are.

Then, holding all your experiences in your senses, gradually allow your consciousness to perceive the floor beneath you. Feel the hardness of the floor. Begin again to sense the differences between the floor and your body.

Let your awareness return to each part of your body, where it lies on the floor. Register your surroundings. Wiggle your fingers and toes. And, when you are ready — and only when you are ready — softly open your eyes. Gently come back into the room.

Stretch your fingers and toes. Then your whole body. And notice how clean, clear and refreshed you feel.

Welcome back!

11

WATER - Sacral Chakra

The sacral chakra is situated about three finger widths below the navel, shining out from where the top of the sacrum or pelvic girdle meets the spine. This chakra spins out towards the front of the body although some clairvoyants see it also emanating from the back. It is the second slowest of the seven major chakras, its frequency so close to that of the base chakra that in some healing modalities they are considered one.

The element to which this chakra relates is Water, and the sense connected with it is the sense of taste. The senses of taste and smell are so intimately connected that one does not function well without the other. The watery secretions of the mouth are vital to the sense of taste. We recognise this when our mouth literally waters when the sense of taste is stimulated — most often by delicious smells emanating from the kitchen!

But water is also changeable and liquid just as our emotions tend to be, constantly changing from one moment to the next.

Thus it follows that this is chakra where perpetual change is normal. Related to it are the kidneys, a paired organ, indicating that this chakra relates to twosomes and partnerships. Since the reproductive organs are also dependent on watery secretions, it follows that such partnerships are often of the emotional and/or romantic kind. It follows, too, that this chakra is concerned with reproduction and creativity as well as with the emotions.

When we 'go with the flow' we allow our emotions to settle of their own accord. This action also reflects our inner strength, for we cannot conquer our emotions by controlling or ignoring them. We need to allow the feeling of the emotion to show us the place in our bodies where we feel unsettled or uncomfortable. Then we can bring our attention to that part of ourselves and then — do nothing. Simply be, breathing into the part where you feel out of balance. Usually the place feels tight and uncomfortable, or perhaps unsettled.

It is easy and familiar to judge the feeling and ourselves. Classic thoughts or words are: 'pull your socks up', 'how could you do that?', 'you should know better'. All of these reactions pull us away from the feeling itself and bring in a great deal of judgement.

Why should we judge ourselves? What is the benefit? To answer the second question first: there are no benefits. And judgement serves no purpose at all. What is the point of it? Better to be aware. If there are things that breed discontent, awareness of them allows us to see them for what they truly are and to take appropriate action.

Remember: feelings are one of the body's ways of

showing where there is an imbalance. Once we know this we can help to rectify the situation.

I suggest that you sit with the feeling/emotion, no matter how raw it may feel. Simply allow it to be there within your body and your energy field. Then begin to 'give it space': imagine the feeling relaxing more and more with each breath: allow it to dissipate and it will gradually fade.

Do not analyse your feelings. Just sit with them, feeling the feelings in your body and becoming aware of the emotions they contain or represent. Like water, emotions ebb and flow, changing constantly.

Emotions and feelings are what give our lives light and shade. Without them, life would be bland. With them, we are open to new experiences and understanding. Celebrate your ability to feel, remembering that sadness is just the other side of happiness. All emotions are just that — emotions — they are not who we are, but they can be powerful if we allow them to be, holding us within a straight-jacket of 'shoulds', 'musts' and 'oughts.' Just for a while, let go of any conditioning — no matter how much it is shrieking for attention — and simply breathe …

Here are three simple ways to experience the Sacral Chakra by bringing your conscious awareness to it. Some take longer than others but all can be accomplished within fifteen minutes. Choose the one that appeals to you most at any given time.

Remember that you may not merge into the Oneness every time you meditate. Indeed it may take a few tries before your mind settles sufficiently to trust the process. And your body too — it is probably unused to stillness.

ONE

A few breaths will help to steady and calm you whatever you are doing or thinking. You may stop doing or thinking ... or you may breathe consciously as you carry on with your daily tasks.

A single conscious breath will work wonders: more slow conscious breaths will calm and relax you and clarify your thinking.

TWO

Breathe out fully ... breathe in deeply ... hold the breath ... and let it go. Breathe out as much as you are able and then breathe out a little more ... breathe in ... and smile! Keep breathing, letting your breath find its own rhythm. Breathe softly into your Sacral Chakra, feel it smiling, and relax. See if any sensations or thoughts drift into your mind ... let them be ... Let nothing change ... only your awareness. Let your awareness linger a few finger-widths below the navel, at the Sacral Chakra ... smile into that chakra.

That is all. You can stay here for as long as you wish,

drifting on the breath, staying comfortably aware of this vital part of yourself.

Or you may wish to use the breath to bring yourself back into everyday consciousness, allowing your awareness to come back to your surroundings.

THREE

A guided meditation, like the one below, is a simple way to find a sense of Oneness if you have 10 to 15 minutes to spare for meditation.

If you wish, you can choose to listen to my voice as it carries you into an awareness of Water and an understanding of the fluidity of this chakra.

WATER MEDITATION
Sacral Chakra

Sit or lie with your back straight. If your back is sore you may lie with a pillow under your knees to take the pressure from your back. Make sure you are comfortable. Stretch and relax each part of your body in turn. If you become aware of tension, take your full attention to that part. Breathe into it. Do not try to change anything. Just allow the tension to be there, acknowledge it and move on.

Take a deep slow breath … and as you breathe out slowly and deeply, become aware of the breath as it passes warmly through your nostrils. As you breathe in feel the slight coolness of the breath and follow it on its journey to your centre. As you breathe out, note its warmth … as you breathe in, note its coolness. Allow the breath to follow its natural pattern …. There is nothing to achieve other than awareness of the breath. There is nothing to do but follow the breath on its slow passage …. In …. And out …. Good.

Allow your breath to become lighter … silent. With each out-breath feel your whole body becoming heavy, heavy, heavy … and relaxed…. Your whole body is relaxed and at ease. Your body is warm: warm and heavy. Heavy and warm … and relaxed.

As you breath out, acknowledge the floor beneath you. Become aware of the places where the floor and your

SPINNING into FORM

body meet. Allow yourself to become one with the floor. Breathe in and breathe out. Softly. Lightly.

As you become one with the floor, allow your body to become lighter, lighter and to float down like a feather on the breeze. Float down, and, as you do so, become aware that you have settled on Water, are floating on Water. You are light and buoyant. And you are floating, floating, on Water. It may be a huge ocean, a warm salty sea, a shallow lake, a hot spring, a boating pond, a paddling pool, or a big puddle — wherever you feel safe.

Now become aware of the smell of the Water.... The briny smell of salt ... the sticky muddy odour of a pond after rain ... the metallic smell of minerals ... or the clean, clear scent of running Water. Become aware of the fragrance all around you, soaking your own scent up from your skin.

Let yourself become aware of the taste of the Water, so close to the way it smells. As you breathe in its scent, hold the taste on your tongue: salt or muddy, metallic or fresh .... Feel relaxed. Relaxed and warm and floaty ....

Hear the small sounds of the Water. The waves softly slapping ... the spray of the spring ... the tinkling sound of running Water ... the slopping sound of the Water against the bank or edge of the pool.

Allow your sense of hearing to become very acute, very clear .... Hear the sound of little fishes swimming beneath you; the sound of water-lilies swaying on the ripples; of plants growing in the Water. Hear the movement of the smallest sea-horse and of each tiny water snail.

See with your inner eye the colour and texture of the Water. There may be huge green ocean rollers, or little tripping twinkling waves on a pond …. Rippling white-crested waves on the blue sea; or tiny brown ripples on the puddle. It may be strong, buoyant and salty; thick and sandy; soft and slimy with mud. It may be bubbling with warmth; or it may be cool and serene. However it is for you, take time to look at it closely … so that you become aware of the micro-organisms that comprise it. The Water that brings life to the Earth.

Turn your attention now to the feel of the Water. Is it cold? Warm? Cool and refreshing? Warm and inviting? Feel how the Water embraces you; completely accepts every part of you. Feel how it supports and encourages you while entering every small crevice of your skin; how it cleans, invigorates … and accepts you as part of it.

Now allow all those sensations to merge in your mind. In your inner being. In your emotions. Sense the feeling, the living being that is Water.

Allow your awareness to encompass all that Water means to you. Whether that is the joy of swimming in it on a warm summers day; or skating on a frozen pond. Whether it is the cool refreshing drink that is "Nature's

Wine"; or the warm relaxing bath that eases away the stresses of the day. Whether it is an invigorating shower in the morning; or the substance that washes away dirt of all sorts — from your skin, from your clothes, from your dishes. Gentle, misty rain or the heavy raindrops of a thunderstorm; banks of snow shining in the winter sun. Or, as you are now, just floating in Water in a relaxed and hazy fashion away from all the cares of the world, allowing them to wash away in the Water … while it supports and nourishes you.

Remember how it is to be a child and play! Just play with the Water in any way you choose: splash it joyfully around you … stamp in it … scoop it up. Let it dribble through your fingers … lap it with your tongue. Wallow in it. Swim in it. Turn cartwheels. Do handstands. Play tag with fishes … or dolphins … or sea-birds. Float dreamily in the sunshine … or dive deeply into the Water. Wonder at the feeling of sheer exuberance … of fun.

Do any, or all, of these things. Or find your own fun. Use Water laughingly and with joy and feel the sheer wonder of its existence. Be aware that we are made of Water. Without it there would be no life.

Give yourself all the time you need to truly experience Water in this moment. And then — when you are ready — take a moment to be grateful. Acknowledge, remember: Water nourishes us, supports us, clears away our negativity … all unnecessary emotions. And balances them so that we are whole, and as capable of joy as we are of sorrow, of love as we are of fear. Let the Water wash away any emotions that you do not need right at this moment. Let any fears or sorrows blend in the Water … and be diluted until they are no longer visible, or tangible. Note, with gratitude, that the Water leaves you happy and clean … clear of all negativity.

If you feel there is still some negativity to clear, you may need a shower; or a bath. Under a waterfall? In a deep pool? Whatever you need, allow yourself to emerge once more shining clean. Full of play: playful. Full of joy: joyful.

Hold that feeling: knowledge; deep knowing; understanding. And now simply accept, know. And understand … on all the levels of your being … from the superficial to the deepest core … that the Water accepts you as you are. There is nothing you have to do … or be … or achieve.

With all your imperfections, you are perfect as you are.

Then, holding all your experiences in your senses, gradually allow your consciousness to perceive the floor beneath you. Feel the hardness of the floor. Begin again to sense the differences between the floor and your body.

Let your awareness return to each part of your body, where it lies on the floor. Register your surroundings. Wiggle your fingers and toes. And, when

SPINNING into FORM

you are ready — and only when you are ready — softly open your eyes. And gently come back into the room.

Stretch your fingers and toes. Then your whole body. And notice how clean, clear and refreshed you feel.

Welcome back!

12

FIRE - Solar Plexus Chakra

The solar plexus chakra is situated above the diaphragm at the point where the sternum ends and the ribs part, shining out like the sun for which it is named. This chakra spins out from the front of the body and less so from the back. This is the centre of our being and the frequency is faster than those of the base and sacral chakras.

The element to which this chakra relates is Fire, and the sense connected with it is the sense of sight. It is the centre of our being, our personal sun, the place from which we shine our light and the chakra of our own personal will and our sense of self. A fire burns brightly, illuminating all before it. But it can also burn too fast, burning itself out. Or it can burn too slowly, easily dowsed by the water of emotion. Sometimes it burns too fiercely, without concern for others or their surroundings; or too weakly, when it is at the mercy of any enemy.

The Solar Plexus Chakra's main function is digestion — the digestion of food, certainly, but also the digestion of ideas, events, happenings, problems, difficulties etcetera. The nature of fire is unpredictability. While we know that fire can be a sudden explosion that spreads fast like the bush fires in Australia, it is helpful to remember that even a slowly burning fuse can ignite a whole barrel of gunpowder. If we allow our fire to go out or to burn too low, we will have no energy for ourselves, no energy to do those things we wish to do, and we will be at the mercy of those who wish to take our power and have us do their bidding. Too often, this can be seen in controlling situations or partnerships where one person strips away the power of another, slowly, (or not so slowly) dowsing their fire.

We need to nurture and feed our personal fire, letting its flames burn away all the dross within us. We need to own our fire and tend it carefully, as we digest all the life experiences through which we pass.

Like water, fire is changeable but it is vital we keep it alight and glowing. It gives us our energy, our juice and our power!

It is deeply connected to the breath. Air fans the embers of a dying fire or cools a fire that has burned too hot. When our fire is out of control, we can experience anger, a need to control, nervousness, anxiety, a fierce possessiveness, a sense of powerlessness, or a red rage.

Again, allow space for the fire to burn. Sit with the feelings and emotions in your body, those feelings and emotions that are connected to the solar plexus and relate to our personal space and our sense of will and of simply being. Allow the fire to be there, accept it and breathe …

Here are three simple ways to experience the Solar Plexus Chakra by bringing your conscious awareness to it. Some take longer than others but all can be accomplished within fifteen minutes. Choose the one that appeals to you most at any given time.

Remember that you may not merge into the Oneness every time you meditate. Indeed it may take a few tries before your mind settles sufficiently to trust the process. And your body too — it is probably unused to stillness.

ONE

A few breaths will help to steady and calm you whatever you are doing or thinking. You may stop doing or thinking … or you may breathe consciously as you carry on with your daily tasks.

A single conscious breath will work wonders: more slow conscious breaths will calm and relax you and clarify your thinking.

TWO

Breathe out fully … breathe in deeply … hold the breath … and let it go. Breathe out as much as you are able and then breathe out a little more … breathe in … and smile! Keep breathing, letting your breath find its own rhythm. Allow your lips to reflect the smile in your Solar Plexus Chakra and relax. See if any sensations or thoughts drift into your mind … let them be … Let nothing change

SPINNING into FORM

… only your awareness. Let your awareness stay around your diaphragm, at the place where your ribs meet at the end of the sternum … at the Solar Plexus Chakra … smile into that chakra.

That is all. You can stay here for as long as you wish, drifting on the breath, staying comfortably aware of this vital part of yourself.

Or you may wish to use the breath to bring yourself back into everyday consciousness, allowing your awareness to come back to your surroundings.

THREE

Or you can read the following words or listen to my voice as it carries you into an awareness of Fire and an understanding of the vibrancy and vitality of this chakra.

FIRE MEDITATION
Solar Plexus Chakra

Sit or lie with your back straight. If your back is sore you may lie with a pillow under your knees to take the pressure from your back. Make sure you are comfortable. Stretch and relax each part of your body in turn. If you become aware of tension, take your full attention to that part. Breathe into it. Do not try to change anything. Just allow the tension to be there, acknowledge it and move on.

Take a deep slow breath … and as you breathe out slowly and deeply, become aware of the breath as it passes warmly through your nostrils. As you breathe in feel the slight coolness of the breath and follow it on its journey to your centre. As you breathe out, note its warmth … as you breathe in, note its coolness. Allow the breath to follow its natural pattern …. There is nothing to achieve other than awareness of the breath. There is nothing to do but follow the breath on its slow passage …. In …. And out …. Good.

Allow your breath to become lighter … silent. With each out-breath feel your whole body becoming heavy, heavy, heavy … and relaxed…. Your whole body is relaxed and at ease. Your body is warm: warm and heavy. Heavy and warm … and relaxed.

As you breath out, acknowledge the floor beneath you. Become aware of the places where the floor and your

body meet. Allow yourself to become one with the floor. Breathe in, softly, lightly. Breathe out, softly, lightly …. Feel your heavy, warm, body sinking into the floor … becoming one with the floor.

As you become one with the floor, allow your body to become lighter. Lighter and warm, very warm and comfortable. Now build yourself a Fire. It may be a small flare from a match, the flame of a lighter or a candle, a camp fire, a warm fire in the grate of your home, or a big bonfire in the garden, or even a huge celebratory beacon complete with fireworks! Build a Fire that makes you comfortable.

Now become aware of the smell of the Fire. The sulphur of the match, the smell of the wood smoke, perhaps the resin from pine-wood, or the sweet aromatic fragrance of apple wood or herbs. Maybe there are pine cones on the Fire … or there may be the dusty smell of coal … or the sharp smell of a fire-lighter, even the tang of gunpowder from the fireworks. Become aware of the smell of smoke all around you…. Feel how it lingers on your skin and in your hair.

Let yourself become aware of the taste of the Fire, of the smoke, so close to the way it smells…. As you breathe in the scent hold the taste on your tongue. Aromatic or dusty: sharp or soft. Or simply familiar: comforting. Feel relaxed … relaxed and warm and comfortable.

Marion Eaton

Hear the sounds of the Fire: the roaring of the flames, or the soft fall of a twig; the rush of air into the heart of the furnace; or the sizzle of wax from the candle. Allow your sense of hearing to become very acute, very clear. Listen to the sound of each little twig as it cackles, the ash as it gently falls or floats aloft, the wick as it burns away. Hear the crack of the coal as it breaks, the hiss of resin burning. Be aware of each separate sound.

With your inner eye note the colour and texture of the Fire. There may be huge red-orange flames and a core or red glowing embers encased in thick hard planks ... or the warm red glow of black coals in the grate. There may be a flickering candle flame with a centre of blue in a yellow flame ... or just the last warm white ashes of a barbecue.

However it is for you, take time to look at it closely ... so that you become aware of the many parts that comprise it: this wonderful Fire that brings warmth and light.

Begin now to concentrate the feel of the Fire, not just the warmth that radiates from it, but the effect it has on your feelings. Does it make you feel warm? Comforted? Cosseted? Relaxed? Or is there any fear within you? Perhaps the fear of being burned, or of a coal jumping from the grate to burn a hole in the carpet? Do you feel exhilarated by the roar of the flames and the smell of the smoke? Are you feeling excited or wary?

SPINNING into FORM

Rejuvenated or full of fun?

Feel the warmth on your skin. Allow the hypnotic dance of the flames to lull you into relaxation and a feeling of "all's well". Become aware of the way in which the Fire burns up all that you throw on it … whether wood, coal or rubbish … as easily as a fever deals with infection. Allow the Fire to become one with you as you watch the dancing flames, and allow it to burn away all but the very core of your being: the essence of who you are. Feel how the Fire entrances you, how it energises every part of you, how it clears away all negativity, all feelings of insecurity, fear, anger, insufficiency…

Now allow all those sensations of smell, of taste, of hearing, seeing, and feeling to merge in your mind … in your inner being … in your emotions. Sense the feeling, the living being, that is Fire. Allow your awareness to encompass all that Fire means to you. Whether that is the joy of lighting a candle for meditation; of sitting beside an open, roaring log fire in a pub, pint in hand; of watching as a huge bonfire is lighted and fireworks light up the sky; or simply making a Fire in the garden at home to clear the garden rubbish. It may be the warm glow of a barbecue, or the gas which cooks the meal. Maybe it is the distant twinkle of a star or the blazing warmth of the sun.

Once again play, as if you were a carefree child! Play with the Fire in any safe way you choose. Watch the pictures that emerge from the flames. Poke a twig into the

Fire and watch as it burns. Stir up the ashes and blow on them to see the embers glow red, and small darting flames appear. Hold out your hands and feet to the warmth it emits. Pour water on the Fire and watch it spit and go out. Run your fingers through the cold silky ashes, or add water to make a lovely mess to wipe all over your hands, face and body. Add more and more rubbish or wood to your Fire and watch it grow huge and light the night sky; watch the gentle rain spitting and skittering across the surface. Walk on it if you dare, knowing you will receive no hurt.

Note that Fire is movement. It is never still until it ceases to be a Fire. Wonder at the feeling of sheer exuberance ... of cleansing. Do any or all of these things ... or find your own way to play. Use Fire with openness and joy and laugh at the power, the aliveness and vitality of it. Be aware that Fire cleanses, gives us our joy in life, it is the energy that drives us, the energy that makes us alive. It brings us light, and without light we would have no life.

Give yourself all the time you need to truly experience Fire in this moment and then — when you are ready — take a moment to be grateful. Acknowledge: remember: that Fire cleanses us, drives us, uses our fuel to create energy within us, helps us digest or dispose of things we no longer require. Let the Fire burn away all but the gold within you, and, in doing so, allow that gold to shine, so that you arise like the phoenix from the ashes, a new and vital being. Give it space to bring you all the joy and vigour you need.

Give thanks for the purifying element of Fire, for its comfort, and for showing you where you have discomfort, for clearing away completely all negativity. Allow yourself to emerge once more hot and bright ... full of warmth. Full of energy: energetic.

Hold that feeling: knowledge; deep knowing; understanding. And now simply accept, know. And understand ... on all the levels of your being — from the superficial to the deepest core — that the Fire accepts you as you are. There is nothing you have to do ... or be ... or achieve.

With all your imperfections, you are perfect as you are.

Then, holding all your experiences in your senses, gradually allow your consciousness to perceive the floor beneath you. Feel the hardness of the floor. Begin again to sense the differences between the floor and your body.

Let your awareness return to each part of your body, where it lies on the floor. Register your surroundings. Wiggle your fingers and toes. And, when you are ready — and only when you are ready — softly open your eyes. And gently come back into the room.

Stretch your fingers and toes. Then your whole body. And notice how clean, clear and refreshed you feel.

Welcome back!

13

AIR - Heart Chakra

The Heart chakra is situated in the centre of the chest at the level of the heart and the fifth of the twelve thoracic vertebrae. Sometimes, tongue in cheek, I call this the 'bra-strap' level. This chakra spins out towards the front of the body although some clairvoyants see it also emanating from the back. It is the gateway between the three lower chakras — which are mostly concerned with our earthly emotional-physical body and our connection to Earth — and the three upper chakras, which are our connection to the Universe and Spirit. As such, the Heart Chakra holds the key to the merging of our physical emotional earthly selves (The Goddess, the Earth Mother) with the energy of the universe (God, the Heavenly Father)

The element to which the Heart chakra relates is Air, and the sense connected with it is the sense of touch. Its main physical function is concerned with the breath and breathing, the only unconscious action that we can also do consciously. But its main purpose is to allow us to feel, understand, and become aware of the nature of unconditional love.

This unconditional love must start with ourselves. Only if we can accept every part of ourselves — exactly as

SPINNING into FORM

we are in each moment — can we offer unconditional love to other beings, both conscious and unconscious, on this planet and beyond. When we link in to the nature of the love — which surrounds us, and which is the unifying force of All-That-Is, the cosmos and the million universes that are present in every tiny speck of dust — only then can we be fully conscious and fully functioning spiritual beings within the temple of our earthly bodies.

Love is in the air. Love is carried on the air that we breathe. We breathe the cosmos' love into our souls and bodies with each in-breath and with each out-breath we send out our own unconditional love to the cosmos and all that has its being in the magnificence of the world around us.

Here are three simple ways to experience the Heart Chakra by bringing your conscious awareness to it. Some take longer than others but all can be accomplished within fifteen minutes. Choose the one that appeals to you most at any given time.

ONE

A few breaths will help to steady and calm you whatever you are doing or thinking. You may stop doing or thinking … or you may breathe consciously as you carry on with your daily tasks.

A single conscious breath will work wonders: more slow conscious breaths will calm and relax you and clarify your thinking.

TWO

Breathe out fully ... breathe in deeply ... hold the breath ... and let it go. Breathe out as much as you are able and then breathe out a little more ... breathe in ... and smile! Keep breathing, letting your breath find its own rhythm. Smile lovingly into your Heart Chakra and relax. See if any sensations or thoughts drift into your mind ... let them be ... Let nothing change ... only your awareness. Let your awareness remain in the centre of your chest at the level of the heart, Feel the beating of your heart as it energises and refreshed the Heart Chakra ... smile into that chakra.

That is all. You can stay here for as long as you wish, drifting on the breath, staying comfortably aware of this vital part of yourself.

Or you may wish to use the breath to bring yourself back into everyday consciousness, allowing your awareness to come back to your surroundings.

THREE

Or you can read the following words or listen to my voice as it carries you into an awareness of Air and an understanding of the unconditional love communicated through this chakra.

AIR MEDITATION
Heart Chakra

Sit or lie with your back straight. If your back is sore you may lie with a pillow under your knees to take the pressure from your back. Make sure you are comfortable. Stretch and relax each part of your body in turn. If you become aware of tension, take your full attention to that part. Breathe into it. Do not try to change anything. Just allow the tension to be there, acknowledge it and move on.

Take a deep slow breath … and as you breathe out slowly and deeply, become aware of the breath as it passes warmly through your nostrils. As you breathe in feel the slight coolness of the breath and follow it on its journey to your centre. As you breathe out, note its warmth … as you breathe in, note its coolness. Allow the breath to follow its natural pattern …. There is nothing to achieve other than awareness of the breath. There is nothing to do but follow the breath on its slow passage …. In …. And out …. Good.

Allow your breath to become lighter … silent. With each out-breath feel your whole body becoming heavy, heavy, heavy … and relaxed…. Your whole body is relaxed and at ease. Your body is warm: warm and heavy. Heavy and warm … and relaxed.

As you breath out, acknowledge the floor beneath you. Become aware of the places where the floor and your

body meet. Allow yourself to become one with the floor. Breathe in, softly, lightly. Breathe out, softly, lightly …. Feel your heavy, warm, body sinking into the floor … becoming one with the floor.

As you become one with the floor, allow your body to become lighter, weightless, as insubstantial as a feather, as wispy as thistledown. Feel yourself rising gently into the Air, becoming one with the Air as you breathe in, remaining one with the Air as you breathe out. You are as soft as thistledown, as thin as gauze, gliding gently on each air current.

Now become aware of the scent of the Air around you. It may be the salty tang of the sea, the fresh smell of ozone … the clean energising smell of oxygen … the soft summer smell of a zephyr breeze … or the earthy, wet smell of the autumn wind. Perhaps you sense the green scent of springtime … or the crisp cold Air of a winter snowfall.

Now allow that scent to grow until you taste it. Let it linger on your tongue: taste it still as you breathe it into your lungs … and as you breathe out, taste the difference..

Hear the sounds of the Air: the gentle fluttering breeze of summer … or the wild autumn wind, bending all the trees and swishing through their branches. Or maybe you hear the winter gales howling round the windows of your home … or leaves softly fluttering in the pale Spring sunshine. Allow your sense of hearing to become very acute, very clear …. Listen to the buzzing of each little insect, the flap of each bird's wings. Be aware of each separate sound.

With your inner eye note the colour and texture of the Air. It may feel tropical, thick with water and the breath of plants; or thin and insubstantial mountain air, full of oxygen and really pure. It may be full of the sweetness of growing things; or arid, dusty, dry. It may seem blue as the sea, or gale green, or yellow with sunshine. It may appear brown or grey or red…. Whatever it is to you, let it be. Take time to look at it closely, so that you become aware of the many parts that comprise it, this wonderful Air that you breathe.

Begin now to concentrate the feel of the Air as it encompasses your being, feel it on your skin, your eyebrows, your lashes. Be aware of the Air as it enters your nostrils, maybe cold and fresh. Notice as it enters your lungs, feel it as you breathe out … warmer now and full of moisture.

Feel the wind in your hair … or the soft caress of the breeze. Perhaps you are aware of a draught that whistles round your feet … or of a gentle Air current on which you can rest as it lifts you ever higher into the blue sky. Let it become one with you, and allow it to lift you … lift your spirits … cleanse and purify you, puffing away all negativity, all that you do not need, the burdens that you have assumed. Allow them all to be blown away by the

Marion Eaton

wind.

Now allow all those sensations of smell, of taste, of hearing, seeing and feeling to merge in your mind, in your inner being, in your emotions. Sense the feeling, the living being that is Air. Allow your awareness to encompass all that Air means to you: whether that is the joy of a light waft of Air on a summer's night, or the exhilaration of a strong wind by the ocean. It may be the feel of the wind in your hair as you ride; or the soft breath of a sleeping child against your cheek; the deep, slow, light breath of meditation; or the urgent panting after strong exercise.

Once again play with the Air, as if you were a carefree child! Simply play with the Air in any way you choose. Fly with the birds, ride a magic carpet, glide gently as thistledown seeking a place to grow; go up in a hot air balloon and drift noiselessly across the sky, as the Air conducts the many and varied sounds to you. Whisk though the sky on the top of clouds scudding across the face of the moon on a windy night. Fly a micro light aeroplane and see clearly through the still summer Air the fields and woods, rivers and villages, perhaps a glimpse of the sea .... Do any, or all, of these things, or find your own way to play in the Air, with the Air. Use it with openness and joy and laugh at the fun and lightness of it. Note that Air is an element in its own right but it is also a vehicle for other elements. Without it nothing could live on this planet. Air consists of elements required by all life; it conducts light, heat, rain and snow. Be aware that the atmosphere around this wonderful planet of ours protects and supports us in a precious and delicate balance between life and nothingness. Air permeates all things. It is the very stuff of life. Without it there would be no life.

Give yourself all the time you need to truly experience Air in all its guises in this moment. And then — when you are ready — take a moment to be grateful, to acknowledge and to remember that Air allows us to breathe; gives us a sense of space; supports and encourages life in all its myriad forms. Let the Air encourage you to dream of all that is possible, let it lighten your experience of life itself, so that you feel light, full of inspiration. Breathe and enjoy it. Give Air time to bring you all the space and the elation you need.

Give thanks for the inspirational element of Air, for its buoyancy, and for showing you where you feel heavy and restricted, for clearing away completely all weighty negativity — those things from which you feel incapable of escape. Allow yourself to become as light and insubstantial and as beautiful as a butterfly, knowing you hold the key to the whole of life in your hand.

Hold that feeling: knowledge; deep knowing; understanding. And now simply accept, know. And understand ... on all the levels of your being — from the superficial to the deepest core — that the Air accepts you as you are. There is nothing you have to do ... or be ... or achieve.

With all your imperfections, you are perfect as you are.

Then, holding all your experiences in your senses, gradually allow your consciousness to perceive the floor beneath you. Feel the hardness of the floor. Begin again to sense the differences between the floor and your body.

Let your awareness return to each part of your body, where it lies on the floor. Register your surroundings. Wiggle your fingers and toes. And, when you are ready — and only when you are ready — softly open your eyes. And gently come back into the room.

Stretch your fingers and toes. Then your whole body. And notice how clean, clear and refreshed you feel.

Welcome back!

14

ETHER - Throat Chakra

The Throat chakra is situated at the base of the neck, in the hollow below the epiglottis or Adam's apple. It is the centre of our creativity and the place from where we speak *our* truth, no matter what that truth may be.

This centre spins outwards, its frequency higher than the Heart Chakra. Now we are moving into the realms of the spiritual, for it is the throat chakra through which we communicate, not only through words on the physical level but through communication with all levels of being, which includes angels, arch-angels, nature spirits and the Earth itself. This list is not exclusive as there are many other levels of communication.

The throat chakra is connected to the ears as well as to the voice. It therefore relates to true hearing, listening, and understanding as well as to speech. Because of this, it is also the centre of creativity. When we really listen to higher understanding and directions we are able to create wonderful things of which our rational selves may be completely ignorant.

Sometimes inspiration comes to us in dreams. This is the centre through which other realms communicate with us and is often easier — because there is less interference from our rational minds — when we are in a semi-conscious state. Many famous inventors, Tesler and Eddison amongst them, have found the answer to conundrums in lucid dreams given to them by this centre; dreams which they have remembered in a conscious state and put to good use.

Our rational mind can block the urgings of the higher intelligence that brings us this information and sometimes we deny the very possibility of receiving important messages 'through the ether'. Funnily enough, the element of this chakra is Ether. Here I use the Ayurvedic term for this amazing energy which is of a substance finer than the gaseous air that we breathe. Ether is space: the space between our joints, inside our sinuses, that is part of each cell in our body. It is the substance in which all the vibrating atoms in our cells move and 'have their being'.

Ether is fine, but it is strong. It is the substance that conveys our thoughts and directions to the autonomic nervous system — the system of which we are not consciously aware, but which controls all aspects of the living life force within us. Bringing awareness to the functioning of this element within our very being allows us to communicate with unseen, unknown realms and to bring their wisdom to our daily lives.

So, once again, I urge you to breathe and to take your full awareness and consciousness to this chakra and this aspect of our being.

SPINNING into FORM

ONE

A few breaths will help to steady and calm you whatever you are doing or thinking. You may stop doing or thinking … or you may breathe consciously as you carry on with your daily tasks.

A single conscious breath will work wonders: more slow conscious breaths will calm and relax you and clarify your thinking.

TWO

Breathe out fully … breathe in deeply … hold the breath … and let it go. Breathe out as much as you are able and then breathe out a little more … breathe in … and smile!

Keep breathing, letting your breath find its own rhythm. Breathe into your Throat Chakra and relax. See if any sensations or thoughts drift into your mind … let them be … Let nothing change … only your awareness. Let your awareness rest at the base of your throat, feel it gently clear any obstruction, large or small … smile into that chakra.

That is all. You can stay here for as long as you wish, drifting on the breath, staying comfortably aware of this vital part of yourself.

Or you may wish to use the breath to bring yourself back into everyday consciousness, allowing your awareness to come back to your surroundings.

THREE

Or you can read the following words or listen to my voice as it carries you into an awareness of Ether and an understanding of the communication and creativity that flow around this chakra.

ETHER MEDITATION
Throat Chakra

Sit or lie with your back straight. If your back is sore you may lie with a pillow under your knees to take the pressure from your back. Make sure you are comfortable. Stretch and relax each part of your body in turn. If you become aware of tension, take your full attention to that part. Breathe into it. Do not try to change anything. Just allow the tension to be there, acknowledge it and move on.

Take a deep slow breath … and as you breathe out slowly and deeply, become aware of the breath as it passes warmly through your nostrils. As you breathe in feel the slight coolness of the breath and follow it on its journey to your centre. As you breathe out, note its warmth … as you breathe in, note its coolness. Allow the breath to follow its natural pattern …. There is nothing to achieve other than awareness of the breath. There is nothing to do but follow the breath on its slow passage …. In …. And out …. Good.

Allow your breath to become lighter … silent. With each out-breath feel your whole body becoming heavy, heavy, heavy … and relaxed…. Your whole body is relaxed and at ease. Your body is warm: warm and heavy. Heavy and warm … and relaxed.

As you breath out, acknowledge the floor beneath you. Become aware of the places where the floor and your

71

body meet. Allow yourself to become one with the floor. Breathe in, softly, lightly. Breathe out, softly, lightly ….

Feel your heavy, warm, body sinking into the floor … becoming one with the floor. As you become one with the floor, allow your body to become lighter, lighter until you feel completely weightless. Breathe softly, gently, silently and become one with your breath.

Watch as your body slowly dissolves into a higher vibration or stays on the floor while your essence changes and becomes finer and finer … as fine as gossamer … as fine as the air you breathe … and then still finer … until you become one with the space between the molecules of gas which make up the air. Feel yourself float between the molecules easily, as if they were clouds of steam, which you could simply blow away. Ether is simply space: the space between all vibrations …between each separate vibration that forms matter. It is the essence from which all things are made, which permeates all things, each molecule, each atom, each neutron, and which connects us with all other things and creatures which have life.

Now become aware of the smell of the Ether. It has almost no fragrance, and that is a smell in itself. It has no earthly counterpart. The absence of scent is free, pure, clean and full of possibilities.

Let yourself become aware of the taste of Ether: but maybe it has none. The absence of taste yet another way to experience it — Ether.

SPINNING into FORM

Maybe you can hear the small sounds of the Ether, as it moves within you, within all things. Or maybe there is an absence of sound. It may be the slight stardust sound of silence: within you, without you. Or it may be the music of the spheres; or the sound of angels voices upraised in unbearably beautiful music. Allow your sense of hearing to become very acute, very clear. Listen to the sound of the space between your joints, the space between each fibre of muscle, between each cell of your body.

See with your inner eye the colour and texture of the Ether. Traditionally it is a beautiful turquoise-blue, or sometimes the blue of a summer sky. Feel how incredibly fine it is. So fine that the eye, the ear, the finger, cannot perceive it. It is beyond the five senses that we use each day here on Earth. But deep within we know that it exists … we can perceive it with the inner eye. It may slip past you at first, it is of such a high vibration. Just focus you inner eye and wait. And it will come to you, like sparkling specks of dust in the sunlight. If you search too hard it may escape your perception, but simply accept and know that it is there. Ether exists as the stuff of dreams, the means of communication between All-That-Is.

Turn your attention now to the feel of Ether as you become one with it. Feel the gossamer fineness of its vibration. It is the "Word" which was in the beginning … the substance that bears all vibration … that permeates and forms part of each nano particle … that forms the waves and spirals upon which, and of which, and in which, all things manifest. Ether is the nothing upon which quantum waves change as they are observed. Feel how Ether embraces you, completely accepts every part of you. Because it *is* part of you: part of each thought, each emotion, each breath you breathe, each cell in your body.

Now allow all those sensations to merge in your mind, in your inner being, in your emotions. Sense the feeling, the living being, that is Ether. Allow your awareness to encompass all that Ether is.

Maybe you can regress in your mind to being a child, a baby, a foetus, a cell, and beyond that to being in spirit before you incarnated. If not, just use your imagination and imagine how it felt to be able to move without the encumbrance of a body. How easy it was, or would be, merely to exist as spirit wafting on the Ether … you could communicate without words and gestures, almost without thinking. Allow your consciousness to expand and to remember. Ride the Ether like a moonbeam … or a sunbeam … or a rainbow. Wonder at the feeling of sheer delight, of simplicity.

Do any or all of these things. Or find your own way to truly experience Ether. Use it laughingly and with joy and feel the sheer wonder of its existence. Be aware that it is the fairy dust of which we are made. It is the very stuff of life.

Give yourself all the time you need to truly

experience Ether in this moment. And then ... when you are ready ... take a moment to nurture gratitude and be grateful, to acknowledge, to remember: that Ether simply 'is'. It encourages us to 'be': to accept ourselves as who we are ...absolutely perfect in this moment, part of the whole of existence. Ether has no other function than to be part of who we are. It is the means through which we communicate with all other beings and objects, animate and inanimate, in the multiverse.

Allow yourself to waft on the Ether through all the positive emotions and feel yourself a being of pure love ... and joy ... and peace.

Hold that feeling: knowledge; deep knowing; understanding. And now simply accept, know ... and understand ... on all the levels of your being — from the superficial to the deepest core — that the Ether accepts you as you are. There is nothing you have to do ... or be ... or achieve.

With all your imperfections, you are perfect as you are.

Then, holding all your experiences in your senses, gradually allow your consciousness to perceive the floor beneath you. Feel the hardness of the floor. Begin again to sense the differences between the floor and your body.

Let your awareness return to each part of your body, where it lies on the floor. Register your surroundings. Wiggle your fingers and toes. And, when you are ready — and only when you are ready — softly open your eyes. And gently come back into the room.

Stretch your fingers and toes. Then your whole body. And notice how clean, clear and refreshed you feel.

Welcome back!

15

LIGHT - Brow Chakra

From the Throat chakra we move upwards on the ether towards the Brow or Third Eye Chakra which lies in the centre of the head: its energy emanates from between the eyebrows. If we close our eyes we can sense this place, a place where a 'third eye' would be if we possessed one.

This centre spins outwards. Its frequency is very high because it is the centre through which we experience our intuition or inner knowing. This is also the chakra of 'mind'.

At the Brow chakra all communication is through the medium of light, vibrating at a speed which makes it almost impossible for the human body to detect. Instead, we understand and interpret it as colour, dreams or visions — and it is interesting that even people who have been blind from birth often experience these phenomena. Sometimes we even say: 'the light dawned' when we receive some information which makes all other things as 'plain as day'.

The Brow Chakra pierces the space between the two hemispheres of the brain, the rational left brain and the intuitive right brain. When we allow a balance here between the two halves of our brain, we allow light to inform each of our cells at a vibrational level far higher than our conscious minds can even imagine. Luckily we have no need to understand or perceive this light — all we need to do is to take our awareness to this centre and meditate on the purest form of light.

Light shines from the oily membrane that surrounds and contains each of our cells. Kirlian and other scientific photography confirm that our energy field is a field of light. This is the chakra through which we experience that light, allowing it to make us whole — healing us at a spiritual level before the energy is stepped down in vibration to serve the lower chakras.

'To those who seek, it shall be given'. If we come to the Light of the brow chakra with trust, humility and openness, the Light itself will reveal to each of us the truth of our being and the joy of existence. Light is a true blessing to those who are prepared to trust in the highest good and the highest realms of communication and vibration.

ONE

To experience light in all its magnificence, we first have to slow our breath and our heartbeat. As you breathe, imagine light filling your lungs as you bring your full conscious awareness to this chakra and this aspect of your being.

SPINNING into FORM

TWO

Breathe out fully … breathe in deeply … hold the breath … and let it go. Breathe out as much as you are able and then breathe out a little more … breathe in … and smile!

Keep breathing, letting your breath find its own rhythm. Smile into your Brow Chakra and relax. See if any sensations or thoughts drift into your mind … let them be … Let nothing change … only your awareness. Let your awareness experience the feeling of this space of the Third Eye at the centre of the brow ridge … smile into that chakra.

That is all. You can stay here for as long as you wish, drifting on the breath, staying comfortably aware of this vital part of yourself.

Or you may wish to use the breath to bring yourself back into everyday consciousness, allowing your awareness to come back to your surroundings.

THREE

Or you can read the following words or listen to my voice as it carries you into an awareness of Light and perhaps a different understanding of the nature of this chakra.

LIGHT MEDITATION
Brow Chakra

Sit or lie with your back straight. If your back is sore you may lie with a pillow under your knees to take the pressure from your back. Make sure you are comfortable. Stretch and relax each part of your body in turn. If you become aware of tension, take your full attention to that part. Breathe into it. Do not try to change anything. Just allow the tension to be there, acknowledge it and move on.

Take a deep slow breath … and as you breathe out slowly and deeply, become aware of the breath as it passes warmly through your nostrils. As you breathe in feel the slight coolness of the breath and follow it on its journey to your centre. As you breathe out, note its warmth … as you breathe in, note its coolness. Allow the breath to follow its natural pattern …. There is nothing to achieve other than awareness of the breath. There is nothing to do but follow the breath on its slow passage …. In …. And out …. Good. Allow your breath to become lighter … silent. With each out-breath feel your whole body becoming heavy, heavy, heavy … and relaxed…. Your whole body is relaxed and at ease. Your body is warm: warm and heavy. Heavy and warm … and relaxed.

As you breath out, acknowledge the floor beneath you. Become aware of the places where the floor and your

body meet. Allow yourself to become one with the floor. Breathe in and breathe out. Softly. Lightly.

Feel your heavy, warm, body sinking into the floor … becoming one with the floor.

As you become one with the floor, allow your body to shine and become lighter … and brighter … brilliant … so brilliant that you outshine the most vivid star you can imagine. Feel yourself breathing Light into your lungs, into each fibre of your body. And as you do so, feel your body dissolve in that Light. Or just sense and know that you are becoming Light and bright and shining; and the fabric of your body is becoming finer and finer; vibrating faster and faster; rarefying more and more … until you are one with Light. Breathe in Light. And, as you exhale, allow the Light to permeate your whole being.

Now take a little while to experience how it feels to be made of Light. Does it have a scent, a perfume? Can you taste it? Does Light have a texture you can experience through the senses of smell and taste? Or is there nothing at all that you can experience through these senses? There are no right answers. Just experience how it is for you, at this moment, when you are made of Light, woven of sunbeams.

Now, turn your attention to your sense of hearing. Can you hear the Light? Can you hear any small or tiny sound connected with it? Perhaps there is a sense of vibration you can pick up with your ears? The music of the spheres perhaps? Or a swishing sound as you whisk through space and time? Maybe there is Light in the sound of your heart beating, or in the air you breathe? Perhaps you can hear it traversing the walls of the cells in your body? Open your physical and subtle ears to the sound of Light … and you will be rewarded with a sensation, and understanding, of the way the subtle body vibrates within Light. Be aware of each aspect of the sound of Light.

Moving now to your sense of sight, become aware that your physical eyes take in Light, which is essential for the smooth running of your body. And with your inner eye observe the colour and texture of the Light. It may be strong and uncomfortable for your physical eyes, as if someone has switched on a light suddenly in the darkness. Or it may be soft and subdued as on a cloudy winter's day. It may be brilliant tropical sun shining on water like a mirror. It may be silver moonlight at the full of the moon; or twinkling stars in frosty sky at the dark of the moon. It may be a candle lighted in the darkness of your meditation room, or the full glare of footlights from a stage. Note the many ways we understand and experience Light. There is Light visible on the darkest night, even if it is just the glimmer of a glow-worm, or the reflected beam from a streetlight. Our eyes adjust even to the black darkness of the deepest cave. And white Light comprises all colours as seen in the prism of the rainbow. Take time

SPINNING into FORM

to look at it closely, so that you become aware of the many parts that comprise it, this amazing vibration of Light.

Begin now to observe how Light feels as it penetrates your entire being. Feel it around you in your aura, on your skin, in your muscles and organs, right through to your bones and the marrow within them. Become aware of the effect Light has on the totality of what you are. Note how it affects your mood. Maybe it lightens you up so that you feel strong, capable, joyful? Or perhaps Light lifts you from a sombre mood? Possibly you take it for granted: so it merely means that you are able to read a good book, cook a wonderful meal, watch television, or write a letter.   Take a moment to consider what life would be like without Light in any form. Your whole body needs Light to survive. Feel how it would be without colour in our lives. Think of the effect of a room painted green … or grey … or orange. Imagine yourself wearing red for a jolly evening, or blue for a calm occasion. Discover the effect of colour … and thus Light … on your skin, your hair, your whole body.

Feel yourself basking in sunlight or dancing barefoot on the grass by moonlight. Really enjoy swathing yourself from top to toe in a single colour or veils of different colours. Feel the effect on your whole essence.

Now allow all these sensations to merge in your mind, in your inner being, in your emotions. Sense the feeling, the living being that is Light. Let Light become one with you, become you, and allow it to lift you, lift your spirits, heal you, making you whole … a creature made of Light, able to communicate through beams of Light.

Just for now, become a child again! Play with the Light, as if you were a child, full of joy and without care. Play with the Light in any way you choose. Paint a picture in different coloured lights. Practise with the footlights, spotlights and filters in the theatre. Fly from star to star … from planet to planet. Ride the rainbow to the furthest part of the universe and see our sun as just a prick of Light. Expand until you are big enough to swallow the moon … and watch it as it flows through your anatomy, illuminating each part of you in turn. Gaze at fireflies dancing over a pond … make a net of Light to attract beautiful moths to you. Use a crystal to catch sunbeams and divide them into fantastic drops of rainbow brightness. See pale green buds and silver catkins on warm brown branches mirrored in a calm lake; and beneath them golden daffodils nodding at their own reflections. Watch as a breeze ripples the water and changes the images.

Do any, or all, of these things, or find your own way to play with Light. Play with openness and fun and laugh at the joy and beauty of it. Note that Light is essential for life. Without it nothing could live on this planet. There would be no food, no warmth, no joy. Be aware that this precious planet of ours literally depends on Light from the sun, to exist. Light protects and supports us in a precious and delicate balance between life and nothing but darkness. It permeates all things. It is the very stuff of life.

Give yourself all the time you need to truly experience Light in all its guises and then — when you are ready — take a moment to acknowledge with thankfulness, to remember, to know fully, that we are made of Light. It is the Light vibration, borne on the ether, that is the womb of life, creating life in all its myriad of forms from air, water, fire and earth. Let the Light encourage you to be aware of all possibilities. Let it fill your lungs as you breathe. Let it give you energy to digest all that life brings you. Light will shine a torch on your fluid ever-changing emotions, and, like lightning, clear all negativity from you. It will allow your roots to grow into the earth, and all your branches to blossom.

Breathe in Light and life and energy. Breathe out Light and life and energy. Surrender yourself totally to the Light and feel the completeness of the love of the Divine encompassing you.

Give thanks for the inspirational element of Light, for its vivacity, its vividness, its radiance — and for illuminating all that is. Allow Light to act as a beacon for all your experiences. Allow it to permeate you and to shine out of your whole life so that you may sparkle, radiating love and Light throughout the world.

Hold that feeling: knowledge; deep knowing; understanding. And now simply accept, know. And understand … on all the levels of your being — from the superficial to the deepest core — that the Light accepts you as you are. There is nothing you have to do … or be … or achieve.

With all your imperfections, you are perfect as you are.

Then, holding all your experiences in your senses, gradually allow your consciousness to perceive the floor beneath you. Feel the hardness of the floor. Begin again to sense the differences between the floor and your body.

Let your awareness return to each part of your body, where it lies on the floor. Register your surroundings. Wiggle your fingers and toes. And, when you are ready — and only when you are ready — softly open your eyes. And gently come back into the room.

Stretch your fingers and toes. Then your whole body. And notice how clean, clear and refreshed you feel.

Welcome back!

16

SPIRIT - Crown Chakra

The Crown chakra, known in Sanskrit as the 'thousand petalled lotus', is different from all the other chakras. Situated on the crown of the head in the place which is open longest before the fontanels finally close together, this 'soft spot' can be easily seen in new-born babies. Often it is pulsing slightly; for it does not close completely until a child is nearing five years of age.

From this spot, a myriad sparkling filaments of energy expand and rise towards the heavens, reaching out into the cosmos like a thousand pulsating sensors — which indeed, they are. This is the centre into which the energy of the universe pours, filtered by the aura and these filaments into a form which we can absorb, interpret with our physical senses and use with our physical body.

This is the centre through which our spiritual self, our soul, enters our body and makes us alive. It is not to be confused with the artificial way that the life force can be kept within the body by machines. This spiritual self, this light body, is the Truth of who we are, being of a much finer energetic substance than the denser energy of the mind and intuition at the Brow Chakra level.

While the Brow Centre seeks to balance our rational

mind 'the ego' with our spacial mind 'the intuition', the Crown Chakra is the funnel for the life force which is known as compassion or supreme love. This is love that asks nothing more than to exist. Even though we may deny it, seeking to use our mind to bring about those things and events we seek — and even though we may be very successful at this during our lifetime — at the end of our time here on Earth within the temple of our spiritual body, it is to Love that we return. For love is the energy of the universe. And spirit is the vehicle for that love to enter our being, the body-mind-spirit that is the physical experience of our presence on Earth.

And so, to Spirit, and through Spirit, we will always return to All-That-Is, the Oneness from which all creation springs.

It can be tempting to abide here at the Crown Chakra, so that we can dismiss the trials of everyday life. But everyday life, with its challenges and rewards are what we are here to experience on this planet. We sell ourselves short if we do not embrace human life and the human condition to the full. Only by doing so can be rise beyond joy and sorrow, into the wonder of 'The One'.

It is possible, as we meditate, to rise still higher in consciousness, but the higher we rise the more uncomfortable it can be to return to everyday awareness — and that we must do in order to complete the lives and

SPINNING into FORM

the purpose for which we took responsibility when we chose to incarnate here on Earth. Breathing helps to anchor us here on earth while we experience all that we are offered by the Creator on the high vibrational level of the Crown Chakra.

ONE

For this reason, practice deep and full breathing to bring you to that place of peace from which you can experience all that there is available to you at this time and in this lifetime.

TWO

Breathe out fully ... breathe in deeply ... hold the breath ... and let it go. Breathe out as much as you are able and then breathe out a little more ... breathe in ... and smile!

Keep breathing, letting your breath find its own rhythm. Smile into your Crown Chakra and relax. See if any sensations or thoughts drift into your mind ... let them be ... Let nothing change ... only your awareness. Feel the myriad of filaments that spread out from your Crown Chakra into the fundament ... smile into the Crown Chakra.

That is all. You can stay here for as long as you wish, drifting on the breath, staying comfortably aware of this vital part of yourself.

Or you may wish to use the breath to bring yourself

back into everyday consciousness, allowing your awareness to come back to your surroundings.

THREE

Or, yet again, you can read the following words — or listen to my voice as it carries you into an overarching awareness of Spirit and allows you to bring back with you experiences that will inform and nourish your life here on Earth.

SPIRIT MEDITATION
Crown Chakra

Sit or lie with your back straight. If your back is sore you may lie with a pillow under your knees to take the pressure from your back. Make sure you are comfortable. Stretch and relax each part of your body in turn. If you become aware of tension, take your full attention to that part. Breathe into it. Do not try to change anything. Just allow the tension to be there, acknowledge it and move on.

Take a deep slow breath … and as you breathe out slowly and deeply, become aware of the breath as it passes warmly through your nostrils. As you breathe in feel the slight coolness of the breath and follow it on its journey to your centre. As you breathe out, note its warmth … as you breathe in, note its coolness. Allow the breath to follow its natural pattern …. There is nothing to achieve other than awareness of the breath. There is nothing to do but follow the breath on its slow passage …. In …. And out …. Good.

Allow your breath to become lighter … silent. With each out-breath feel your whole body becoming heavy, heavy, heavy … and relaxed…. Your whole body is relaxed and at ease. Your body is warm: warm and heavy. Heavy and warm … and relaxed.

As you breath out, acknowledge the floor beneath you. Become aware of the places where the floor and your

body meet. Allow yourself to become one with the floor. Breathe in softly, lightly … and breathe out softly, lightly.

Feel your heavy, warm, body sinking into the floor … becoming one with the floor.

As you become one with the floor, allow yourself to become lighter, weightless. Feel yourself drifting in the air … rising higher and higher into the ether … rising still higher and higher until you are beyond the world of manifestation, in that beautiful warm darkness where all possibilities begin … in the womb of all creation, safe warm, protected. Allow your body to dissolve into the velvet blackness of the void. Here there is no negativity, there is no pain, no struggle, no emotional trauma. You simply are ….

Now take a little while to experience how it feels to be made of nothingness, of pure Spirit. Here you have no need of earthly senses: smell, taste, sight, sound, feeling. They are so heavy that they simply drop away from you. They have no place in this world of Spirit. You do not need a body, you simply have to wish to be somewhere — and you are there. Or to be something — and so you become. Or to know something — and that knowledge is instantly yours.

Here there is no separation. You become part of all things. All things are part of you.

Take a moment or two now to simply experience:

How it is to have no needs … for all your needs are

met.

How it is to have no striving. There is nothing to strive for … because you can have anything, everything … *be* anything, everything.

How it is to be part of all that is … part of the web of eternal life.

How it is to be at one with all things, all vibration — whether light, ether, sound, air, fire, water, earth — all that has life.

How it is to lie in the womb of creation and feel warm, safe, protected.

How it is to be fully seen, fully accepted, and completely loved — exactly as you are in this moment.

Allow the experience to become part of you, as you begin to allow yourself to be drawn back to earth. Be fully aware of the possibilities open to you. Be aware that you have simply to decide how much of this experience you wish to bring back to the world. You can bring it all or you can bring a tiny part — or even nothing at all. There are truly all possibilities. You have the power to choose, and the ability to translate those choices into reality, to manifest your dearest desires.

What do you bring with you? Perhaps a scent, a perfume? Can you taste it? Does Spirit have a texture you can experience through the senses? Does it have a sound? Or a feeling? What does it look like? There are no right answers. Just experience how it is for you, at this moment, as you bring your consciousness back slowly into this dear world of ours.

Maybe you will hold onto that sense of belonging, of rightness, of choice, of creativity.

Whatever it is, begin now to bring it slowly back into your body, feel yourself returning through your crown chakra, and as you do so, allow yourself to separate from All-That-Is, to condense into a stream of white light pouring in through in through the crown of your head.

Allow that light to separate into rainbow colours as the vibrational level becomes gradually slower. Watch as each colour stops within your body; and as it does so, become aware of that body part, manifesting itself once more on the earth.

Indigo spirals at the brow centre: the colour of midnight on a tropical island. Become aware of your head, all the bones of it, the muscles, the brain, the blood vessels, the spaces of your sinuses, your eyes. The capacity to see, to take in light.

Blue sifts down to your throat centre: the colour of a cloudless summer sky. Become aware of your ears, your mouth, your tongue, your jaw, your teeth, your throat, and your neck. The capacity to communicate on all levels of your being, listening to your intuition, to simply know, to speak and express yourself truly, just as you are

Green gently lodges at the heart centre: the colour of bright, spring leaves and soft pink dog roses blowing in a country hedge. Become aware of your shoulders, your chest, your lungs, and the spaces within where you are nourished by breathing the light vibrational essence of air, each bronchiole and each tiny air sack. Become aware of your heart, that wonderful pump which beats all our lives, ensuring that the energy of the breath spreads throughout our being. The capacity to love in all senses of the word, from your favourite food, to the knowledge of being a part of each and every living thing. The power and kindness of compassion.

Yellow stops at the Solar plexus centre: the colour of daffodils, of winter jasmine, of the sun. Become aware of all your digestive organs, stomach, pancreas, liver, spleen, and of your backbone. All of them lend you power, feed the energy that you need to exist on the earth plane, to hold you upright. The capacity for enthusiasm, for spontaneity, for sharing your joy, the capacity to take your own decisions, 'to hoe your own row', whatever form they take.

Orange glows in the sacral chakra: the colour of oranges, marigolds, of Buddhist Monks' clothes. Let orange light soak into your pelvis. As it does so, become aware of the bones of the pelvic girdle, your sacrum, your hips, and of the basin within containing your intestines and your reproductive organs. The capacity for all the emotional ups and downs, but particularly for fun, laughter and sharing. The ability to digest and create from all of life's experiences.

And finally red passes down into the base chakra at the base of the spine. The colour of glowing embers in a fire on a dismal day, of ladybirds, and the iridescence of butterflies' wings. Red shines its warming, comforting light through the pubic bone and the coccyx, down the legs, thighs, shins, calves, ankles and into the feet. Red grounds you in security, bringing the capacity to move forward … from a place of safety … into uncertainty, wrapped in a warm cloak of confidence.

Give yourself all the time you need to truly experience yourself once more, to become aware of each part of your body and then allow the light to carry on down from your feet to root you into the earth, so that you are once more fully aware of your body and of the earth.

You realise now that you are a creature of the earth, but also a spiritual being with roots in the heavens, just like the Tree of Life. You hold the secret of the universe within each cell of your being.

Give thanks and allow gratitude to flow into every corner of your body, your mind, your emotions, and your soul.

Hold that feeling: knowledge; deep knowing; understanding. And now simply accept, know. And understand … on all the levels of your being … from the superficial to the deepest core … that you are fully seen, fully known, fully accepted and fully loved exactly as you are. There is nothing you have to do … or be … or achieve.

With all your imperfections, you are perfect as you are.

Then, holding all your experiences in your senses, gradually allow your consciousness to perceive the floor beneath you. Feel the hardness of the floor. Begin again to sense the differences between the floor and your body.

Let your awareness return to each part of your body, where it lies on the floor. Register your surroundings. Wiggle your fingers and toes. And, when you are ready — and only when you are ready — softly open your eyes. And gently come back into the room.

Stretch your fingers and toes. Then your whole body. And notice how clean, clear and refreshed you feel.

Welcome back!

17

JOURNEY through the Chakras

Several people have asked to have all the chakra meditations in one long journey from Earth at the Base Chakra to Spirit at the Crown. So here I have gathered all the meditations into one to form a journey through the chakras.

JOURNEY THROUGH THE CHAKRAS
MEDITATION

Sit or lie with your back straight. If your back is sore you may lie with a pillow under your knees to take the pressure from your back. Make sure you are comfortable. Stretch and relax each part of your body in turn. If you become aware of tension, take your full attention to that part. Breathe into it. Do not try to change anything. Just allow the tension to be there, acknowledge it and move on.

Take a deep slow breath ... and as you breathe out slowly and deeply, become aware of the breath as it passes warmly through your nostrils. As you breathe in feel the slight coolness of the breath and follow it on its journey to your centre. As you breathe out, note its warmth ... as you

SPINNING into FORM

breathe in, note its coolness. Allow the breath to follow its natural pattern …. There is nothing to achieve other than awareness of the breath. There is nothing to do but follow the breath on its slow passage …. In …. And out …. Good.

Allow your breath to become lighter … silent. With each out-breath feel your whole body becoming heavy, heavy, heavy … and relaxed…. Your whole body is relaxed and at ease. Your body is warm: warm and heavy. Heavy and warm … and relaxed.

As you breath out, acknowledge the floor beneath you. Become aware of the places where the floor and your body meet. Allow yourself to become one with the floor. Breathe in and breathe out. Softly. Lightly.

Feel your heavy, warm, body sinking into the floor … becoming one with the floor.

As you become one with the floor, allow your body to melt into it. And become aware that the floor has changed its texture. It is warm and it is soft. It is mud … Earth: warm, soft, supportive Earth. Feel how it holds you … supports you … nourishes you … like a mother holding her child warmly to her breast.

Feel the sensation of the Earth against your skin.

Now become aware of the smell of the Earth: the soft muddy odour of the Earth after rain; the intense primeval smell.

Feel the scent all around you, soaking your own scent up from your skin.

Marion Eaton

Let yourself become aware of the taste of the Earth: so close to its smell… As you breathe in the scent, hold its taste on your tongue ….

Feel relaxed … relaxed and warm and Earthy…..

Hear the small sounds of the Earth: soft, sticky sounds perhaps. Or the dry flicking sound of dust. Allow your sense of hearing to become very still … very acute … very clear.

Hear the sound of water deep within the Earth: the sound of plant roots growing down into the Earth: Listen to the movement of each infinitesimally small insect and each tiny worm.

See with your inner eye the texture of the Earth. It may be soft, slimy mud: it may be hard and dusty. Or it may be a warm, fine, tilth just ready for the seed to be planted.

However it is for you, take time to look at it closely, so that you become aware of the micro-organisms that comprise it: the soil, the Earth.

Now allow all those sensations to merge in your mind … in your inner being … in your emotions. Sense the feeling, the living being, that is Earth.

Allow your awareness to encompass all that Earth means to you. Whether that is the joy of lying on it on a warm summer's day; or striding through muddy puddles on a walk down a farm track. Whether it is striding up a hill, or climbing a mountain. Clinging to rocks, or running barefoot in the sand. Digging a flowerbed, or making mud pies as a child.

Be a child! Play with the Earth in any way that takes your fancy. Taste it; chew it; smooth it with your hands, your toes. Make mud pies … or sandcastles. Rub dirt into your hair. Let soil dribble through your fingers … allow it to become soft and bathe in it. Smear it all over your skin … smother yourself in mud. Do any, or all, of these things; or find your own fun. Use it laughingly and with joy and feel the sheer wonder of its existence.

Be aware that Earth is the foundation of all life. We are truly children of the Earth.

… Give yourself all the time you need to truly experience Earth in this moment. And then — when you are ready — take a moment to give thanks. To acknowledge … to remember … that the Earth takes all our negativity; takes all our unnecessary waste; the manure of our bodies; the toxicity of our emotions — and sanitises them. Commutes them, and transforms them to soil in which beautiful plants can grow.

Let go of all your negativity … physical … mental … emotional. Let it seep into the Earth for transformation, transmutation. Into the Earth, with gratitude. Leaving you happy and clean, clear of all negativity.

If you feel dirty or muddy, you may need a shower. Or a bath. Under a waterfall, in a deep pool. Whatever your needs, allow yourself to emerge shining clean. Full of delight: delightful. Full of joy: joyful.

Hold that feeling: knowledge; deep knowing; understanding. And now simply accept, know … and understand … on all the levels of your being — from the superficial to the deepest core — that the Earth accepts you as you are.

Now allow your body to become lighter, lighter and to float down like a feather on the breeze. Float down, and, as you do so, become aware that you have settled on Water, are floating on Water. You are light and buoyant. And you are floating, floating, on Water. It may be a huge ocean, a warm salty sea, a shallow lake, a hot spring, a boating pond, a paddling pool, or a big puddle — wherever you feel safe.

Now become aware of the smell of the Water…. The briny smell of salt … the sticky muddy odour of a pond after rain … the metallic smell of minerals … or the clean, clear scent of running Water. Become aware of the fragrance all around you, soaking your own scent up from your skin.

Let yourself become aware of the taste of the Water, so close to the way it smells. As you breathe in its scent, hold the taste on your tongue: salt or muddy, metallic or fresh …. Feel relaxed. Relaxed and warm and floaty ….

Hear the small sounds of the Water. The waves

softly slapping … the spray of the spring … the tinkling sound of running Water … the slopping sound of the Water against the bank or edge of the pool.

Allow your sense of hearing to become very acute, very clear …. Hear the sound of little fishes swimming beneath you; the sound of water-lilies swaying on the ripples; of plants growing in the Water. Hear the movement of the smallest sea-horse and of each tiny water snail.

See with your inner eye the colour and texture of the Water. There may be huge green ocean rollers, or little tripping twinkling waves on a pond …. Rippling white-crested waves on the blue sea; or tiny brown ripples on the puddle. It may be strong, buoyant and salty; thick and sandy; soft and slimy with mud. It may be bubbling with warmth; or it may be cool and serene. However it is for you, take time to look at it closely … so that you become aware of the micro-organisms that comprise it. The Water that brings life to the Earth.

Turn your attention now to the feel of the Water. Is it cold? Warm? Cool and refreshing? Warm and inviting? Feel how the Water embraces you; completely accepts every part of you. Feel how it supports and encourages you while entering every small crevice of your skin; how it cleans, invigorates … and accepts you as part of it.

Now allow all those sensations to merge in your mind. In your inner being. In your emotions. Sense the feeling, the living being that is Water.

Allow your awareness to encompass all that Water means to you. Whether that is the joy of swimming in it on a warm summers day; or skating on a frozen pond. Whether it is the cool refreshing drink that is "Nature's Wine"; or the warm relaxing bath that eases away the stresses of the day. Whether it is an invigorating shower in the morning; or the substance that washes away dirt of all sorts — from your skin, from your clothes, from your dishes. Gentle, misty rain or the heavy raindrops of a thunderstorm; banks of snow shining in the winter sun. Or, as you are now, just floating in Water in a relaxed and hazy fashion away from all the cares of the world, allowing them to wash away in the Water ... while it supports and nourishes you.

Remember how it is to be a child and play! Just play with the Water in any way you choose: splash it joyfully around you ... stamp in it ... scoop it up. Let it dribble through your fingers ... lap it with your tongue. Wallow in it. Swim in it. Turn cartwheels. Do handstands. Play tag with fishes ... or dolphins ... or sea-birds. Float dreamily in the sunshine ... or dive deeply into the Water. Wonder at the feeling of sheer exuberance ... of fun.

Do any, or all, of these things. Or find your own fun. Use Water laughingly and with joy and feel the sheer wonder of its existence. Be aware that we are made of Water. Without it there would be no life.

SPINNING into FORM

Give yourself all the time you need to truly experience Water in this moment. And then — when you are ready — take a moment to be grateful. Acknowledge, remember: Water nourishes us, supports us, clears away our negativity … all unnecessary emotions. And balances them so that we are whole, and as capable of joy as we are of sorrow, of love as we are of fear. Let the Water wash away any emotions that you do not need right at this moment. Let any fears or sorrows blend in the Water … and be diluted until they are no longer visible, or tangible. Note, with gratitude, that the Water leaves you happy and clean … clear of all negativity.

If you feel there is still some negativity to clear, you may need a shower; or a bath. Under a waterfall? In a deep pool? Whatever you need, allow yourself to emerge once more shining clean. Full of play: playful. Full of joy: joyful.

Hold that feeling: knowledge; deep knowing; understanding. And now simply accept, know. And understand … on all the levels of your being … from the superficial to the deepest core … that the Water accepts you as you are.

Now … allow your body to become lighter. Lighter and warm, very warm and comfortable. Now build yourself a Fire. It may be a small flare from a match, the flame of a lighter or a candle, a camp fire, a warm fire in the grate of your home, or a big bonfire in the garden, or even a huge celebratory beacon complete with fireworks! Build a Fire that makes you comfortable.

Now become aware of the smell of the Fire. The sulphur of the match, the smell of the wood smoke, perhaps the resin from pine-wood, or the sweet aromatic fragrance of apple wood or herbs. Maybe there are pine cones on the Fire … or there may be the dusty smell of coal … or the sharp smell of a fire-lighter, even the tang of gunpowder from the fireworks. Become aware of the smell of smoke all around you…. Feel how it lingers on your skin and in your hair.

Let yourself become aware of the taste of the Fire, of the smoke, so close to the way it smells…. As you breathe in the scent hold the taste on your tongue. Aromatic or dusty: sharp or soft. Or simply familiar: comforting. Feel relaxed … relaxed and warm and comfortable.

Hear the sounds of the Fire: the roaring of the flames, or the soft fall of a twig; the rush of air into the heart of the furnace; or the sizzle of wax from the candle. Allow your sense of hearing to become very acute, very clear. Listen to the sound of each little twig as it cackles, the ash as it gently falls or floats aloft, the wick as it burns away. Hear the crack of the coal as it breaks, the hiss of resin burning. Be aware of each separate sound.

With your inner eye note the colour and texture of

the Fire. There may be huge red-orange flames and a core or red glowing embers encased in thick hard planks ... or the warm red glow of black coals in the grate. There may be a flickering candle flame with a centre of blue in a yellow flame ... or just the last warm white ashes of a barbecue.

However it is for you, take time to look at it closely ... so that you become aware of the many parts that comprise it: this wonderful Fire that brings warmth and light.

Begin now to concentrate the feel of the Fire, not just the warmth that radiates from it, but the effect it has on your feelings. Does it make you feel warm? Comforted? Cosseted? Relaxed? Or is there any fear within you? Perhaps the fear of being burned, or of a coal jumping from the grate to burn a hole in the carpet? Do you feel exhilarated by the roar of the flames and the smell of the smoke? Are you feeling excited or wary? Rejuvenated or full of fun?

Feel the warmth on your skin. Allow the hypnotic dance of the flames to lull you into relaxation and a feeling of "all's well". Become aware of the way in which the Fire burns up all that you throw on it ... whether wood, coal or rubbish ... as easily as a fever deals with infection. Allow the Fire to become one with you as you watch the dancing flames, and allow it to burn away all but the very core of your being: the essence of who you are. Feel how the Fire entrances you, how it energises every part of you, how it clears away all negativity, all feelings of insecurity, fear, anger, insufficiency…

Now allow all those sensations of smell, of taste, of hearing, seeing, and feeling to merge in your mind … in your inner being … in your emotions. Sense the feeling, the living being, that is Fire. Allow your awareness to encompass all that Fire means to you. Whether that is the joy of lighting a candle for meditation; of sitting beside an open, roaring log fire in a pub, pint in hand; of watching as a huge bonfire is lighted and fireworks light up the sky; or simply making a Fire in the garden at home to clear the garden rubbish. It may be the warm glow of a barbecue, or the gas which cooks the meal. Maybe it is the distant twinkle of a star or the blazing warmth of the sun.

Once again play, as if you were a carefree child! Play with the Fire in any safe way you choose. Watch the pictures that emerge from the flames. Poke a twig into the Fire and watch as it burns. Stir up the ashes and blow on them to see the embers glow red, and small darting flames appear. Hold out your hands and feet to the warmth it emits. Pour water on the Fire and watch it spit and go out. Run your fingers through the cold silky ashes, or add water to make a lovely mess to wipe all over your hands, face and body. Add more and more rubbish or wood to your Fire and watch it grow huge and light the night sky; watch the gentle rain spitting and skittering across the surface. Walk on it if you dare, knowing you will receive no hurt.

Note that Fire is movement. It is never still until it ceases to be a Fire. Wonder at the feeling of sheer exuberance ... of cleansing. Do any or all of these things ... or find your own way to play. Use Fire with openness and joy and laugh at the power, the aliveness and vitality of it. Be aware that Fire cleanses, gives us our joy in life, it is the energy that drives us, the energy that makes us alive. It brings us light, and without light we would have no life.

Give yourself all the time you need to truly experience Fire in this moment and then — when you are ready — take a moment to be grateful. Acknowledge: remember: that Fire cleanses us, drives us, uses our fuel to create energy within us, helps us digest or dispose of things we no longer require. Let the Fire burn away all but the gold within you, and, in doing so, allow that gold to shine, so that you arise like the phoenix from the ashes, a new and vital being. Give it space to bring you all the joy and vigour you need.

Give thanks for the purifying element of Fire, for its comfort, and for showing you where you have discomfort, for clearing away completely all negativity. Allow yourself to emerge once more hot and bright ... full of warmth. Full of energy: energetic.

Hold that feeling: knowledge; deep knowing; understanding. And now simply accept, know. And understand … on all the levels of your being — from the superficial to the deepest core — that the Fire accepts you as you are.

Let your body become lighter, weightless, as insubstantial as a feather, as wispy as thistledown. Feel yourself rising gently into the Air, becoming one with the Air as you breathe in, remaining one with the Air as you breathe out. You are as soft as thistledown, as thin as gauze, gliding gently on each air current.

Now become aware of the scent of the Air around you. It may be the salty tang of the sea, the fresh smell of ozone … the clean energising smell of oxygen … the soft summer smell of a zephyr breeze … or the earthy, wet smell of the autumn wind. Perhaps you sense the green scent of springtime … or the crisp cold Air of a winter snowfall.

Now allow that scent to grow until you taste it. Let it linger on your tongue: taste it still as you breathe it into your lungs … and as you breathe out, taste the difference..

Hear the sounds of the Air: the gentle fluttering breeze of summer … or the wild autumn wind, bending all the trees and swishing through their branches. Or maybe you hear the winter gales howling round the windows of your home … or leaves softly fluttering in the pale Spring sunshine. Allow your sense of hearing to become very acute, very clear …. Listen to the buzzing of each little insect, the flap of each bird's wings. Be aware of each separate sound.

With your inner eye note the colour and texture of the Air. It may feel tropical, thick with water and the breath of plants; or thin and insubstantial mountain air, full of oxygen and really pure. It may be full of the sweetness of growing things; or arid, dusty, dry. It may seem blue as the sea, or gale green, or yellow with sunshine. It may appear brown or grey or red.... Whatever it is to you, let it be. Take time to look at it closely, so that you become aware of the many parts that comprise it, this wonderful Air that you breathe.

Begin now to concentrate the feel of the Air as it encompasses your being, feel it on your skin, your eyebrows, your lashes. Be aware of the Air as it enters your nostrils, maybe cold and fresh. Notice as it enters your lungs, feel it as you breathe out ... warmer now and full of moisture.

Feel the wind in your hair ... or the soft caress of the breeze. Perhaps you are aware of a draught that whistles round your feet ... or of a gentle Air current on which you can rest as it lifts you ever higher into the blue sky. Let it become one with you, and allow it to lift you ... lift your spirits ... cleanse and purify you, puffing away all negativity, all that you do not need, the burdens that you have assumed. Allow them all to be blown away by the wind.

Marion Eaton

Now allow all those sensations of smell, of taste, of hearing, seeing and feeling to merge in your mind, in your inner being, in your emotions. Sense the feeling, the living being that is Air. Allow your awareness to encompass all that Air means to you: whether that is the joy of a light waft of Air on a summer's night, or the exhilaration of a strong wind by the ocean. It may be the feel of the wind in your hair as you ride; or the soft breath of a sleeping child against your cheek; the deep, slow, light breath of meditation; or the urgent panting after strong exercise.

Once again play with the Air, as if you were a carefree child! Simply play with the Air in any way you choose. Fly with the birds, ride a magic carpet, glide gently as thistledown seeking a place to grow; go up in a hot air balloon and drift noiselessly across the sky, as the Air conducts the many and varied sounds to you. Whisk though the sky on the top of clouds scudding across the face of the moon on a windy night. Fly a micro light aeroplane and see clearly through the still summer Air the fields and woods, rivers and villages, perhaps a glimpse of the sea …. Do any, or all, of these things, or find your own way to play in the Air, with the Air. Use it with openness and joy and laugh at the fun and lightness of it. Note that Air is an element in its own right but it is also a vehicle for other elements. Without it nothing could live on this planet. Air consists of elements required by all life; it conducts light, heat, rain and snow. Be aware that the atmosphere around this wonderful planet of ours protects and supports us in a precious and delicate balance between life and nothingness. Air permeates all things. It is the very stuff of life. Without it there would be no life.

Give yourself all the time you need to truly experience Air in all its guises in this moment. And then — when you are ready — take a moment to be grateful, to acknowledge and to remember that Air allows us to breathe; gives us a sense of space; supports and encourages life in all its myriad forms. Let the Air encourage you to dream of all that is possible, let it lighten your experience of life itself, so that you feel light, full of inspiration. Breathe and enjoy it. Give Air time to bring you all the space and the elation you need.

Give thanks for the inspirational element of Air, for its buoyancy, and for showing you where you feel heavy and restricted, for clearing away completely all weighty negativity — those things from which you feel incapable of escape. Allow yourself to become as light and insubstantial and as beautiful as a butterfly, knowing you hold the key to the whole of life in your hand.

Hold that feeling: knowledge; deep knowing; understanding. And now simply accept, know. And understand … on all the levels of your being — from the superficial to the deepest core — that the Air accepts you as you are.

Marion Eaton

Allow your body to become lighter, lighter until you feel completely weightless. Breathe softly, gently, silently and become one with your breath.

Watch as your body slowly dissolves into a higher vibration or stays on the floor while your essence changes and becomes finer and finer ... as fine as gossamer ... as fine as the air you breathe ... and then still finer ... until you become one with the space between the molecules of gas which make up the air. Feel yourself float between the molecules easily, as if they were clouds of steam, which you could simply blow away. Ether is simply space: the space between all vibrations ...between each separate vibration that forms matter. It is the essence from which all things are made, which permeates all things, each molecule, each atom, each neutron, and which connects us with all other things and creatures which have life.

Now become aware of the smell of the Ether. It has almost no fragrance, and that is a smell in itself. It has no earthly counterpart. The absence of scent is free, pure, clean and full of possibilities.

Let yourself become aware of the taste of Ether: but maybe it has none. The absence of taste yet another way to experience it — Ether.

Maybe you can hear the small sounds of the Ether, as it moves within you, within all things. Or maybe there is an absence of sound. It may be the slight stardust sound of silence: within you, without you. Or it may be the music of the spheres; or the sound of angels voices upraised in unbearably beautiful music. Allow your sense of hearing to become very acute, very clear. Listen to the sound of the space between your joints, the space between each fibre of muscle, between each cell of your body.

See with your inner eye the colour and texture of the Ether. Traditionally it is a beautiful turquoise-blue, or sometimes the blue of a summer sky. Feel how incredibly fine it is. So fine that the eye, the ear, the finger, cannot perceive it. It is beyond the five senses that we use each day here on Earth. But deep within we know that it exists … we can perceive it with the inner eye. It may slip past you at first, it is of such a high vibration. Just focus you inner eye and wait. And it will come to you, like sparkling specks of dust in the sunlight. If you search too hard it may escape your perception, but simply accept and know that it is there. Ether exists as the stuff of dreams, the means of communication between All-That-Is.

Turn your attention now to the feel of Ether as you become one with it. Feel the gossamer fineness of its vibration. It is the "Word" which was in the beginning … the substance that bears all vibration … that permeates and forms part of each nano particle … that forms the waves and spirals upon which, and of which, and in which, all things manifest. Ether is the nothing upon which quantum waves change as they are observed. Feel how Ether embraces you, completely accepts every part of you. Because it *is* part of you: part of each thought, each emotion, each breath you breathe, each cell in your body.

Now allow all those sensations to merge in your mind, in your inner being, in your emotions. Sense the feeling, the living being, that is Ether. Allow your awareness to encompass all that Ether is.

Maybe you can regress in your mind to being a child, a baby, a foetus, a cell, and beyond that to being in spirit before you incarnated. If not, just use your imagination and imagine how it felt to be able to move without the encumbrance of a body. How easy it was, or would be, merely to exist as spirit wafting on the Ether … you could communicate without words and gestures, almost without thinking. Allow your consciousness to expand and to remember. Ride the Ether like a moonbeam … or a sunbeam … or a rainbow. Wonder at the feeling of sheer delight, of simplicity.

Do any or all of these things. Or find your own way to truly experience Ether. Use it laughingly and with joy and feel the sheer wonder of its existence. Be aware that it is the fairy dust of which we are made. It is the very stuff of life.

Give yourself all the time you need to truly experience Ether in this moment. And then … when you are ready … take a moment to nurture gratitude and be grateful, to acknowledge, to remember: that Ether simply 'is'. It encourages us to 'be': to accept ourselves as who we are …absolutely perfect in this moment, part of the whole of existence. Ether has no other function than to be part of who we are. It is the means through which we communicate with all other beings and objects, animate and inanimate, in the multiverse.

Allow yourself to waft on the Ether through all the positive emotions and feel yourself a being of pure love … and joy … and peace.

Hold that feeling: knowledge; deep knowing; understanding. And now simply accept, know … and understand … on all the levels of your being — from the superficial to the deepest core — that the Ether accepts you as you are.

Now feel as your body begins to shine and become lighter … and brighter … brilliant … so brilliant that you outshine the most vivid star you can imagine. Feel yourself breathing Light into your lungs, into each fibre of your body. And as you do so, feel your body dissolve in that Light. Or just sense and know that you are becoming Light and bright and shining; and the fabric of your body is becoming finer and finer; vibrating faster and faster; rarefying more and more … until you are one with Light. Breathe in Light. And, as you exhale, allow the Light to permeate your whole being.

Now take a little while to experience how it feels to be made of Light. Does it have a scent, a perfume? Can you taste it? Does Light have a texture you can experience through the senses of smell and taste? Or is there nothing at all that you can experience through these senses? There are no right answers. Just experience how it is for you, at this moment, when you are made of Light, woven of sunbeams.

Now, turn your attention to your sense of hearing. Can you hear the Light? Can you hear any small or tiny sound connected with it? Perhaps there is a sense of vibration you can pick up with your ears? The music of the spheres perhaps? Or a swishing sound as you whisk through space and time? Maybe there is Light in the sound of your heart beating, or in the air you breathe? Perhaps you can hear it traversing the walls of the cells in your body? Open your physical and subtle ears to the sound of Light … and you will be rewarded with a sensation, and understanding, of the way the subtle body vibrates within Light. Be aware of each aspect of the sound of Light.

Moving now to your sense of sight, become aware that your physical eyes take in Light, which is essential for the smooth running of your body. And with your inner eye observe the colour and texture of the Light. It may be strong and uncomfortable for your physical eyes, as if someone has switched on a light suddenly in the darkness. Or it may be soft and subdued as on a cloudy winter's day. It may be brilliant tropical sun shining on water like a mirror. It may be silver moonlight at the full of the moon; or twinkling stars in frosty sky at the dark of the moon. It may be a candle lighted in the darkness of your meditation room, or the full glare of footlights from a stage. Note the many ways we understand and experience Light. There is Light visible on the darkest night, even if it is just the glimmer of a glow-worm, or the reflected beam from a streetlight. Our eyes adjust even to the black darkness of the deepest cave. And white Light comprises all colours as seen in the prism of the rainbow. Take time to look at it closely, so that you become aware of the many parts that comprise it, this amazing vibration of Light.

Begin now to observe how Light feels as it penetrates your entire being. Feel it around you in your aura, on your skin, in your muscles and organs, right through to your bones and the marrow within them. Become aware of the effect Light has on the totality of what you are. Note how it affects your mood. Maybe it lightens you up so that you feel strong, capable, joyful? Or perhaps Light lifts you from a sombre mood? Possibly you take it for granted: so it merely means that you are able to read a good book, cook a wonderful meal, watch television, or write a letter. Take a moment to consider what life would be like without Light in any form. Your whole body needs Light to survive. Feel how it would be without colour in our lives. Think of the effect of a room painted green ... or grey ... or orange. Imagine yourself wearing red for a jolly evening, or blue for a calm occasion. Discover the effect of colour … and thus Light … on your skin, your hair, your whole body.

Feel yourself basking in sunlight or dancing barefoot on the grass by moonlight. Really enjoy swathing yourself from top to toe in a single colour or veils of different colours. Feel the effect on your whole essence.

Now allow all these sensations to merge in your mind, in your inner being, in your emotions. Sense the feeling, the living being that is Light. Let Light become one with you, become you, and allow it to lift you, lift your spirits, heal you, making you whole … a creature made of Light, able to communicate through beams of Light.

Just for now, become a child again! Play with the Light, as if you were a child, full of joy and without care. Play with the Light in any way you choose. Paint a picture in different coloured lights. Practise with the footlights, spotlights and filters in the theatre. Fly from star to star … from planet to planet. Ride the rainbow to the furthest part of the universe and see our sun as just a prick of Light. Expand until you are big enough to swallow the moon … and watch it as it flows through your anatomy, illuminating each part of you in turn. Gaze at fireflies dancing over a pond … make a net of Light to attract beautiful moths to you. Use a crystal to catch sunbeams and divide them into fantastic drops of rainbow brightness. See pale green buds and silver catkins on warm brown branches mirrored in a calm lake; and beneath them golden daffodils nodding at their own reflections. Watch as a breeze ripples the water and changes the images.

Do any, or all, of these things, or find your own way to play with Light. Play with openness and fun and laugh at the joy and beauty of it. Note that Light is essential for life. Without it nothing could live on this planet. There would be no food, no warmth, no joy. Be aware that this precious planet of ours literally depends on Light from the sun, to exist. Light protects and supports us in a precious and delicate balance between life and nothing but darkness. It permeates all things. It is the very stuff of life.

Give yourself all the time you need to truly experience Light in all its guises and then — when you are ready — take a moment to acknowledge with thankfulness, to remember, to know fully, that we are made of Light. It is the Light vibration, borne on the ether, that is the womb of life, creating life in all its myriad of forms from air, water, fire and earth. Let the Light encourage you to be aware of all possibilities. Let it fill your lungs as you breathe. Let it give you energy to digest all that life brings you. Light will shine a torch on your fluid ever-changing emotions, and, like lightning, clear all negativity from you. It will allow your roots to grow into the earth, and all your branches to blossom.

Breathe in Light and life and energy. Breathe out Light and life and energy. Surrender yourself totally to the Light and feel the completeness of the love of the Divine encompassing you.

Give thanks for the inspirational element of Light, for its vivacity, its vividness, its radiance — and for illuminating all that is. Allow Light to act as a beacon for all your experiences. Allow it to permeate you and to shine out of your whole life so that you may sparkle, radiating love and Light throughout the world.

Hold that feeling: knowledge; deep knowing; understanding. And now simply accept, know. And understand … on all the levels of your being — from the superficial to the deepest core — that the Light accepts you as you are.

Feel yourself becoming lighter, weightless. Feel yourself drifting in the air … rising higher and higher into the ether … rising still higher and higher until you are beyond the world of manifestation, in that beautiful warm darkness where all possibilities begin … in the womb of all creation, safe warm, protected. Allow your body to dissolve into the velvet blackness of the void. Here there is no negativity, there is no pain, no struggle, no emotional trauma. You simply are ….

Now take a little while to experience how it feels to

be made of nothingness, of pure Spirit. Here you have no need of earthly senses: smell, taste, sight, sound, feeling. They are so heavy that they simply drop away from you. They have no place in this world of Spirit. You do not need a body, you simply have to wish to be somewhere — and you are there. Or to be something — and so you become. Or to know something — and that knowledge is instantly yours.

Here there is no separation. You become part of all things. All things are part of you.

Take a moment or two now to simply experience:

How it is to have no needs … for all your needs are met.

How it is to have no striving. There is nothing to strive for … because you can have anything, everything … *be* anything, everything.

How it is to be part of all that is … part of the web of eternal life.

How it is to be at one with all things, all vibration — whether light, ether, sound, air, fire, water, earth — all that has life.

How it is to lie in the womb of creation and feel warm, safe, protected.

How it is to be fully seen, fully accepted, and completely loved — exactly as you are in this moment.

Allow the experience to become part of you, as you begin to allow yourself to be drawn back to earth. Be fully aware of the possibilities open to you. Be aware that you have simply to decide how much of this experience you wish to bring back to the world. You can bring it all or you can bring a tiny part — or even nothing at all. There are truly all possibilities. You have the power to choose, and the ability to translate those choices into reality, to manifest your dearest desires.

What do you bring with you? Perhaps a scent, a perfume? Can you taste it? Does Spirit have a texture you can experience through the senses? Does it have a sound? Or a feeling? What does it look like? There are no right answers. Just experience how it is for you, at this moment, as you bring your consciousness back slowly into this dear world of ours.

Maybe you will hold onto that sense of belonging, of rightness, of choice, of creativity.
Whatever it is, begin now to bring it slowly back into your body, feel yourself returning through your crown chakra, and as you do so, allow yourself to separate from All-That-Is, to condense into a stream of white light pouring in through in through the crown of your head.

Allow that light to separate into rainbow colours as the vibrational level becomes gradually slower. Watch as each colour stops within your body; and as it does so, become aware of that body part, manifesting itself once more on the earth.

Indigo spirals at the brow centre: the colour of

midnight on a tropical island. Become aware of your head, all the bones of it, the muscles, the brain, the blood vessels, the spaces of your sinuses, your eyes. The capacity to see, to take in light.

Blue sifts down to your throat centre: the colour of a cloudless summer sky. Become aware of your ears, your mouth, your tongue, your jaw, your teeth, your throat, and your neck. The capacity to communicate on all levels of your being, listening to your intuition, to simply know, to speak and express yourself truly, just as you are

Green gently lodges at the heart centre: the colour of bright, spring leaves and soft pink dog roses blowing in a country hedge. Become aware of your shoulders, your chest, your lungs, and the spaces within where you are nourished by breathing the light vibrational essence of air, each bronchiole and each tiny air sack. Become aware of your heart, that wonderful pump which beats all our lives, ensuring that the energy of the breath spreads throughout our being. The capacity to love in all senses of the word, from your favourite food, to the knowledge of being a part of each and every living thing. The power and kindness of compassion.

Yellow stops at the Solar plexus centre: the colour of daffodils, of winter jasmine, of the sun. Become aware of all your digestive organs, stomach, pancreas, liver, spleen, and of your backbone. All of them lend you power, feed the energy that you need to exist on the earth plane, to hold you upright. The capacity for enthusiasm, for spontaneity, for sharing your joy, the capacity to take your own decisions, 'to hoe your own row', whatever form they take.

Orange glows in the sacral chakra: the colour of oranges, marigolds, of Buddhist Monks' clothes. Let orange light soak into your pelvis. As it does so, become aware of the bones of the pelvic girdle, your sacrum, your hips, and of the basin within containing your intestines and your reproductive organs. The capacity for all the emotional ups and downs, but particularly for fun, laughter and sharing. The ability to digest and create from all of life's experiences.

And finally red passes down into the base chakra at the base of the spine. The colour of glowing embers in a fire on a dismal day, of ladybirds, and the iridescence of butterflies' wings. Red shines its warming, comforting light through the pubic bone and the coccyx, down the legs, thighs, shins, calves, ankles and into the feet. Red grounds you in security, bringing the capacity to move forward … from a place of safety … into uncertainty, wrapped in a warm cloak of confidence.

Give yourself all the time you need to truly experience yourself once more, to become aware of each part of your body and then allow the light to carry on down from your feet to root you into the earth, so that you are once more fully aware of your body and of the earth.

SPINNING into FORM

You realise now that you are a creature of the earth, but also a spiritual being with roots in the heavens, just like the Tree of Life. You hold the secret of the universe within each cell of your being.

Give thanks and allow gratitude to flow into every corner of your body, your mind, your emotions, and your soul.

Hold that feeling: knowledge; deep knowing; understanding. And now simply accept, know. And understand … on all the levels of your being … from the superficial to the deepest core … that you are fully seen, fully known, fully accepted and fully loved exactly as you are. There is nothing you have to do … or be … or achieve.

With all your imperfections, you are perfect as you are.

Then, holding all your experiences in your senses, gradually allow your consciousness to perceive the floor beneath you. Feel the hardness of the floor. Begin again to sense the differences between the floor and your body.

Let your awareness return to each part of your body, where it lies on the floor. Register your surroundings. Wiggle your fingers and toes. And, when you are ready — and only when you are ready — softly open your eyes. And gently come back into the room.

Stretch your fingers and toes. Then your whole body. And notice how clean, clear and refreshed you feel.

Welcome back!

18

An End and a Beginning

And so we come to the end of this slim volume. I hope that it has proved a useful tool to deepen your personal experience of your subtle energy in general, and of the seven major chakras in particular.

I wish you joy and happiness in your journey back to the stars — from which we have all come and to which we shall all return. May you also find deep spiritual peace and a knowledge of your own special gifts.

Om shanti: may peace be with you.

May you never doubt the value of your life and of your unique contribution to All-That-Is.

Namasté: the Divine in me sees the Divine in you.

Acknowledgements

First, I thank my many, many inspirational teachers — those who first encouraged me to open to my spiritual life by introducing me to Osho's wisdom, and those who have inspired and informed me along my way. Some I have met in person, some in spirit, some over the internet, and others between the pages of their books. They are too many to thank individually and yet each has given me a gift which I will appreciate forever. My grateful thanks.

Special thanks go to all my Reiki students, who have taught me so much about how little I know, and who have encouraged me to give voice to the understanding I have reached. May you all be richly blessed.

Particular thanks to Rebekah Sperring for her help with editing this book. Any faults that remain are entirely mine.

To those clients who have trusted that I have the tools to help them on some part of their journey through life, I offer my deep appreciation. It is your trust and commitment to your own healing that has allowed me to heal parts of myself on my own journey to wholeness. You have held up a mirror and shown me much. May you, too, be blessed; and may you find the wholeness and happiness you seek.

To the many people who have helped me on my way through life, I offer my sincere thanks. Many are my dear friends, all are fellow travellers, some have merely crossed my path fleetingly. For all the lessons learned and

Marion Eaton

understanding gleaned, I thank you.

The gestation period for this offering of mine has been a long one — somewhere in the region of fifteen years — and throughout that time my husband, Richard Eaton, has been incredibly supportive, cheering me on until the final word was written and recorded. And then encouraging me onwards through the (apparently never-ending) editing, proofing, and uploading processes. Thank you, Richard. I could not have done it without you.

But most of all, thank you, my readers and listeners for inviting me into your lives. I feel your energy, and your connection to me and to the Infinite. I am grateful beyond words to you all for joining me on this fascinating journey. May we all find that which we are seeking — and may the quest be full of incident, love, compassion and laughter.

About the Author

Marion Eaton became a Usui Reiki Master in 1994 and a Karuna Reiki® Master in 1996 and has taught Reiki to hundreds of students over the years. She is also a qualified lawyer, aromatherapist, massage therapist and Reiki practitioner. All forms of holistic health interest her and she has studied many different modalities over the years. However, it is energy healing, in all its various facets and forms, which she finds most fascinating and from which she can never quite retire.

She now lives in the Sussex countryside with a very understanding husband, a very spoiled and lazy hound and a large rambling garden, all of which she attempts to keep in some semblance of order.

More information can be found at marioneaton.com.

A note from the Author

Thank you very much for reading my words. I do hope you enjoyed travelling the meditative path with me and that you found something within these pages that resonates with your own understanding.

If you would like to receive the occasional newsletter, please sign up for one on marioneaton.com. You may also like to follow me on Twitter @marioneaton and/or like my Facebook page. I would love to hear from you. Please mention this book and I will be pleased to send you a free short story in appreciation.

You may not know that honest reviews are of immense value to an author so if you would leave one at amazon.co.uk, and amazon.com I will be very appreciative. Thank you.

Other Books published by Touchworks Ltd
The Elephants' Choice
By **M.L. Eaton**

It is 1954 and Melanie is six years old. With her parents, she moves to Bombay, India, where her father has been posted to undertake a Civil Engineering project but, anxious and unsettled, she finds it difficult to make friends.

Entranced by the emotive beauty of her surroundings, she unexpectedly discovers the love and friendship that banish her loneliness.

Always enthralling and exhilarating, at times sad and poignant, this is a story that captures the wonders of India as seen through the eyes of a young English girl.

Readers' Reviews:

'Having read this novella in one sitting as it was, quite literally, 'unputdownable'; I would love to recommend it most highly to other readers. The prose is almost poetic, if that observation is allowed in technical English language terms! It is strongly evocative of the sounds, smells and culture of the Indian sub continent in the dying days of the British influence. Sad in parts, ultimately it was a most uplifting story of a child's awakening to the world outside her sheltered existence.'

'This is a delightful book and a joy to read.'

'This is a beautiful book - the language is rich and evocative and the story immensely touching and insightful whilst exploring themes of love and loss from different perspectives of the adults and the child ... and the elephants. There is also a deeper wisdom to be found between the lines. I loved it and was sad to finish it.'

'An enchanting evocation of childhood years spent in India.'

When the Clocks Stopped
by **M.L. Eaton**

No 1 in the Mysterious Marsh Series

The long hot summer of 1976. The mysterious Romney Marsh in the South of England. Hazel Dawkins, a feisty young lawyer, takes maternity leave anticipating a period of tranquillity. Instead, the dreams begin. In them she encounters Annie, a passionate young woman whose romantic and tempestuous life was adventurously lived, more than two centuries previously, in the cottage that Hazel now occupies.

As their destinies entwine, Hazel not only confronts a terrifying challenge which parallels history, she finds herself desperately fighting for survival in a cruel and unforgiving age. Even more disturbing is the realisation that her battle will affect the future for those in the past whose fate is, as yet, unwritten.

Her only ally is Annie. Together they face events that echo through the centuries, events that are as violent and compelling as they are unexpected.

And, as the past collides with the present, the time for the birth of Hazel's child draws ever nearer.

When the Tide Turned
by **M.L. Eaton**

No 2 in the Mysterious Marsh Series

It is August 1976 and an oppressive heat hangs over Romney Marsh in the South East corner of England.

Soon after the birth of her daughter, Hazel Dawkins, a young lawyer, is unexpectedly asked to return to work. No sooner has she agreed than she discovers that a dark force threatens both her family and her country; and before long, the past and present intertwine in a rising tide of horrifying events.

Haunted by terrifying images, she knows that she must uncover secrets from the past if she is to avert a catastrophe that will destroy all that she holds dear.

What draws her to the painting depicting a sudden storm at sea on a night in 1803 as Napoleon prepares to invade England?

What is the secret of the man pegged down to die on the incoming tide?

As Hazel seeks the answers to these questions, she faces evil and intrigue, her life and that of her baby daughter, threatened at every turn.

A Taste of

When the Clocks Stopped

Prologue

The silver light of a gibbous moon shimmers on the new green leaves of the ash tree. The horse stamps and jerks his head, jangling the bridle. I sway with the movement, soothing him instinctively. The sweetish smell of horse is thick about me as I wait at the crossroads. Stiff as I am in every joint and sinew, my body screams for me to dismount and stretch my legs, but I cannot. Some intuition, some sense of impending destiny, holds me motionless. I am aware it will not be long.

I flinch as the expectant hush is broken by the screech of an owl, eerie in the stillness that binds me to the saddle. She circles silently above me, seeking her prey. I watch until she glides away into the blackest shadows, where the sacred ash grove huddles beneath the escarpment.

My eyes seek the hallowed place where the Earth Mother is still honoured by man and maid on the sacred feast of Beltane; the ash grove to which they come at dawn, clad in white, and garlanded in green. May blossoms wreathe their brows as they stand side by side under a living canopy for their hand-clasping, their ceremony of rejoicing in union, the celebration of life itself in dance and song. This is the seven-treed sacred grove to which my beloved and I came not long ago; there we swore an oath to honour our love and there later, alone beneath the moon-silvered leaves we became one in the flesh.

It grows cold now, and I shiver. The horse pricks up his ears, listening intently. A small sound trembles towards me; perhaps no more than a fluctuation in the air current. Then the nightingale's exquisite song fills the air with beauty. It is the signal:Jack's signal.

I fire my weapon into the sky and wheel about, pulling sharply on the reins. We race off into the night. Lying close to the horse's back, my head beside his ear, I ride hard. For a moment or two, as we gather speed, I choose those places where the low light gleams through the covering of cloud. I catch the sound of hooves in swift pursuit and know I have been seen. Now I guide my good companion into the gloom of the darkest shadows, allowing him to choose his own footing on the causeway. He gallops on.

I risk a backward glimpse. Shapes pursue us; legless in the mist rising from the Marsh, centaurs ride hard in a bow-shaped line. The triumph and excitement of the men who chase me is almost palpable. How long were they lingering near the crossroads where I myself had waited?

I let the gelding have his head because he knows these levels well. His hooves drum into the earth and I crouch low in the saddle, horse sweat hot-smelling in my nostrils. As I cling to his mane, I chance another glance but see nothing. I am sure we are gaining on our pursuers, but have they ridden yet into the trap where the Marsh is quicksand and will swallow horse and rider whole?

The moon is hidden now and I have no bearings. All I hear is a thrumming, thrumming, thrumming — and I know not whether it is my heart beating in my ears or the sound of pursuit. All I can do is ride.

www.ingramcontent.com/pod-product-compliance
Lightning Source LLC
Chambersburg PA
CBHW051002060726

47593CB00017B/730